SACRAMENTS

PAPERS OF THE MAYNOOTH UNION
SUMMER SCHOOLS

The Church, the Body of Christ, according to St Paul by Conleth Kearns, O.P., Dominican Publications: Dublin 1960, and

Membership of the Mystical Body by Patrick J. Hamell, Browne & Nolan: Dublin 1958. Selections from the papers of the 1957 session on "The Mystical Body of Christ".

Mother of the Redeemer, edited by Kevin McNamara, Gill & Son: Dublin 1959; Sheed & Ward: New York 1960. Papers of the 1958 session.

Preaching, edited by Ronan Drury, Gill & Son: Dublin 1962; Sheed & Ward: New York 1963. Papers of the 1960 session.

Christian Unity, edited by Kevin McNamara, The Furrow Trust, Gill & Son: Dublin 1962. Papers of the 1961 session.

The Meaning of Christian Marriage, edited by Enda McDonagh, The Furrow Trust, Gill & Son: Dublin 1963; Alba House: New York 1964. Papers of the 1962 session.

SACRAMENTS

Papers of the Maynooth Union
Summer School 1963

Edited by
DENIS O'CALLAGHAN

THE FURROW TRUST

GILL & SON, DUBLIN

First published 1964 by
M. H. Gill and Son Limited
50 Upper O'Connell Street
Dublin 1
in association with
The Furrow Trust
Maynooth

© *The Furrow Trust 1964*

PRINTED IN THE REPUBLIC OF IRELAND AT THE
LEINSTER LEADER, NAAS.

CONTENTS

CONTRIBUTORS

THE REVEREND LOUIS BOUYER, CONG. ORAT., is the author of many books and articles on liturgical and theological subjects.

THE REVEREND JOSEPH CUNNANE, D.D., is engaged in pastoral work in Balla, Co. Mayo.

THE REVEREND CORNELIUS ERNST, O.P., S.T.L., M.A., teaches in Hawkesyard Priory, Rugeley, Staffordshire.

THE REVEREND SEAN FAGAN, S.M., S.T.L., D.Ph., is Superior of Mount St Mary's, Milltown.

THE REVEREND THOMAS MARSH, D.D., is Professor of Dogmatic Theology, St John's College, Waterford.

THE REVEREND KEVIN MCNAMARA, D.D., is Professor of Dogmatic Theology, St Patrick's College, Maynooth.

THE REVEREND DENIS O'CALLAGHAN, D.D., D.C.L., is Professor of Moral Theology, St Patrick's College, Maynooth.

THE REVEREND KEVIN O'DOHERTY, D.D., is a member of the Maynooth Mission to China, St Columban's, Navan.

THE REVEREND DERMOT RYAN, L.S.S., M.A., is Professor of Oriental Languages, University College, Dublin.

INTRODUCTION

THE decades since the war, marked by such <u>advances in the profane sciences</u>, have been years of quest and challenge in theology also—not least in the field of sacramental doctrine. Accepted attitudes have been re-examined, explanations have been questioned—not because they are "old" <u>(truth is never old)</u>, but because they are seen to be <u>incomplete</u> in the light of further knowledge and awareness, and because their time-worn expression is found to be <u>devoid of any particular appeal to the contemporary mind.</u> This trend towards renewal through self-examination is a sign of health and buoyancy. Indeed, its absence would give cause for the greatest alarm.

The mystery of Christ is greater than any human statement or expression of it. To deny this by adhering blindly to a particular formulation as absolute and complete is to deny the very mystery. <u>Truth itself is one</u>, ever old and ever new, <u>but man's possession of it at any particular time while valid is necessarily imperfect.</u> Again, a stable terminology is essential for science, but if theology becomes hedged by formulae and closed to new insights one finds oneself in the position of the integrist of de Lubac's *Paradox*, ". . . not clinging to the old, but possibly, quite simply, to what is antiquated".

The reader will forgive me for these observations on trends and topics which have been so much in the news over the past months. I mention them here because they are of special interest to the theology of the sacraments. If there was ever a strong temptation to rest content with the statement of a doctrine at a particular high-point of its development, this temptation has been yielded to in regard to the Counter Reformation teaching on the sacraments.

<u>The Fathers of Trent never intended to draw up an exhaustive statement of the Catholic teaching in this province.</u> Shortage of time and the very circumstances of the Council defined the terms of their undertaking. The heretical teachings of the Reformers, especially Luther's *De Captivitate Babylonica*, threw long shadows over their meetings. In its well-known series of canons the Council explicitly condemned the chief Protestant errors, but even in its more positive decrees these errors were continually before its mind. After Trent these same influences were still at work. The spur of controversy is not the best stimulus to a balanced theology,

since over-emphasis on certain aspects inevitably leads to under-statement of others, and one can never satisfactorily define the Catholic thesis in terms of the antithesis.

Certainly, the definitions of the Council of Trent remain, and will ever remain, dogmatically infallible. No Catholic theologian can ever question that the sacraments are in themselves *ex opere operato* causes of grace. But the constant underlining of this point without reference to the wider background may easily give the impression that the sacraments are merely, or chiefly, static rites which automatically transfer their charge of grace on the fulfil-ment of certain extrinsic conditions on the part of the subject. In the satisfaction of working out the mechanics of the sacrament it is so easy to lose sight of the essential mystery—that the sacra-ment is the organic extension of Christ's saving humanity where the Christian meets his Lord as personally and as effectively as the apostles did on the shores of the Sea of Galilee; that the sacra-ment as it affects the individual is nothing less than the sacrament of the Church in action, the community of the mystical body bringing forth and perfecting its members; that the faith, hope and charity of the subject are an intrinsic element in the sacra-ment's saving efficacy, because we are justified not as things but as persons whose free-will under grace is expected to respond in the fullest degree to the approach of Christ.

In the first constitution promulgated by Vatican II, namely, the decree on the Liturgy, we see the Church under the guidance of the Holy Spirit setting out to restore the balance. There is no question of denying previous teaching; she simply brings to the fore aspects which have remained in the background for polemical or other reasons.

In Trent it was decreed: "If anyone shall say that the sacraments were instituted *only* for the purpose of nourishing faith, let him be anathema" (c. 5). But theologians locked in controversy had no immediate interest in the admission implicit in the *only*; their most urgent task was to establish that the sacraments were direct causes of grace. Naturally, so as to highlight the native causality of the rite, they chose as the typical sacrament that in which the dispositions were at a minimum. In the circumstances this was perfectly understandable, but the consequences were unfortunate—it tended to show the sacrament as an impersonal, material source of grace and led one to believe that there were "two ways" of salvation, namely, personal and sacramental holiness. But as Scripture constantly teaches, justification is achieved by the inner unity of faith and sacrament. Obviously the above attitude could be corrected by reflection—but why should one have to reflect? If the doctrinal emphasis were correct, the attitude would necessarily be so. The balance is redressed in the constitution on the Liturgy:

> The sacraments are ordained to the sanctification of men, to the building up of the Body of Christ, to the worship of God; as signs also they have a place in instruction. They not only pre-suppose faith, but they nourish, strengthen and express it by word and action; therefore are they called the sacraments of faith. They do indeed confer grace, but their celebration disposes the faithful most efficaciously for a fruitful reception, for the worship of God, and for the exercise of charity (n. 59).

The phrase "*sacramenta fidei*" was used by St Thomas and the scholastics right up to the Council of Trent; for obvious reasons it was eschewed by the theologian intent on shoring up Catholic doctrine against Luther and Calvin. The phrase underlines the basic truth that the sacraments are living signs rather than things —expressions of that living belief and worship of the Church which give them their full meaning as symbolic actions; expressions of the recipient's initial movement of response to Christ which the innate power of the sacrament as an act of Christ perfects. This may dispel the mistaken idea that the sacraments afford an easy way to salvation, or that they demand nothing more than that one does not place an obstacle to their innate efficacy.

Again, the Counter Reformation's concentration on the sacramental rite in itself (see the whole series of canons in Trent) tended to allow its "background", the perspective of Christ, to appear of lesser importance. But Christ not only won the grace of justification, he not only instituted the sacraments, he is active in them here and now. It is no distortion to say that this is the true meaning of *ex opere operato*—as Melchior Cano penetratingly pointed out in the debates at Trent, St Thomas discarded this formula in the *Summa* although he had consistently used it in the *Commentary*, but he discarded it in favour of the parallel "*ex opere Christi*", "*in virtute Christi*".

The sacrament is in truth the extension (*instrumentum separatum*) of Christ's humanity (*instrumentum coniunctum*); as a visible sign it continues the incarnation of the Word. The sacrament not only brings the grace of Christ, it also brings the Christian face to face with Christ. This is the mystery of the sacrament; it achieves the most real contact possible between the God of heaven and the man of earth. To the believer the sacrament is not a veil hiding the face of Christ, rather is it the very condition of his revelation. The word of Scripture and the action of the sacrament intertwine to bring about this divine revelation or encounter—the words explain the action and give it its complete signification, the action realizes the words and educes their full efficacy. Here, too, we may quote the above constitution with its echoes of *Mediator Dei*:

> To accomplish this tremendous work Christ is always present with his Church, especially in the liturgical actions. He is present in the sacrament of the Mass both in the person of the minister and particularly in the eucharistic species. He is present by his power in the sacraments, so that when anyone baptizes, it is Christ who baptizes. He is present in his word, since it is he who speaks when the sacred Scriptures are read in the Church (n. 7).

The papers of the Maynooth Union Summer School 1963 here published try to present in true perspective some of these valuable insights into the doctrine of the sacraments. The reader will doubtless note that here, as in other provinces, "new theology" is something of a misnomer and, indeed, a source of much misunderstanding. Father Schillebeeckx of Nijmegen, who will be quoted so frequently in these pages, came to formulate his "modern" sacramental theology through a close study of biblical, patristic and Thomistic teaching. There is question then, at least to a great extent, of a renewal by a return to the sources —on the old glossator's advice: "*Aqua purior manat a fonte quam per rivos*".

DENIS O'CALLAGHAN

Sacraments Foreshadowed

DERMOT RYAN

THE aim of this paper is to draw attention to some aspects of Old Testament thought and practice which are relevant to a complete understanding of the sacramental system of the New Law. It is hoped that this consideration of God's use of material things to effect the salvation of Israel may throw light on some features of the New Testament sacraments which for one reason or another have become obscured.[1]

With this purpose in mind, we should turn to the first verse of the book of Genesis, not so much for the sake of beginning at the beginning as to find a statement which is fundamental to the sacramental systems of the Old and the New Law: "In the beginning God created the heavens and the earth". These first words of Holy Writ seldom make an impact on adults who have grown up with them and have always lived in the security of the truth they express. This very security may mean that such readers are rarely stimulated to plumb the depths of their meaning. Here it is not relevant to discuss the meaning of the words "in the beginning" and the attendant question whether the Israelites

---

[1] Those who wish to have an up-to-date discussion of the Christian significance of the Old Testament and the attendant problems concerning typology and allegory should read P. Grelot's *Sens Chrétien de l'Ancien Testament*, Tournai 1962.

wished to express by these words *creatio ex nihilo* or not. Attention should rather be focused on the rest of the verse: God created the heavens and the earth. It sometimes happens in tracts on creation that the words "heaven and earth" are completely emptied of their pictorial content and one is given as an equivalent: *omnia*. "*Deus creavit coelum et terram, quod significat: Deus creavit omnia*".

The Hebrew writer, however, meant to convey far more than the rather abstract *omnia* when he wrote his sentence as is clear from the subsequent account of creation. The heavens for him were the setting for the great lights of heaven, the sun and moon, as well as their lesser companions, the stars. In their regular movements across the sky, the heavenly bodies regulated the days and weeks, the months and the years. Their movements governed the movements of men and animals, even making life and activity possible.[2] From the flood-gates of the firmament of heaven poured down the life-giving waters and the fertile dew which moistened the arid earth.

"The earth" of *Genesis* 1:1 was an earth which is productive of things which are good. Contrasted with the heavens, it included the dry land which brought forth in due season luscious grass and fruitful trees, as well as the waters which teemed with fish.[3] It was this earth too which in response to God's fertile word produced animals and all things that creep on the face of the earth. God beholding the heavens and the earth, with their ceaseless motion and teeming life saw that they were good, and fit to be given to the greatest of his creatures, man.[4]

The splendid ease of God's creative activity and his majestic independence contrast with the boisterous labours of the pagan god-teams, and set the God of Israel above all the gods of the nations. The God of Israel was the author and origin of all creation, which was a work of such stupendous power that the

---

[2] Cf. *Ps.* 103:19; *Eccles.* 9:9-10.
[3] *Gen.* 1:2.
[4] *Gen.* 1 *passim*; *Ps.* 8.

Israelites loved to invoke him under the title: Yahweh, the creator of the heavens and the earth:[5]

> Come, let us sing joyfully to Yahweh;
>   let us acclaim the rock of our salvation.
> Let us greet him with thanksgiving;
>   let us joyfully sing psalms to him.
> For Yahweh is a great God,
>   and a great king above all gods;
> In his hands are the depths of the earth,
>   and the tops of the mountains are his.
> His is the sea, for he has made it,
>   and the dry land, which his hands have formed.
>
> Come, let us bow down in worship;
>   let us kneel before Yahweh who made us.
> For he is our God,
>   and we are the people he shepherds, the flock he guides.
>   *Ps.* 94:1-7.[6]

The whole of creation, as if aware of its relation to God, declares his glory to the ends of the earth and rejoices that it is the product of God's love.[7] The twinkling stars in their silent courses and the sun in his blazing path chant the glory of God's handiwork in a song without words:

> The heavens declare the glory of God,
>   and the firmament proclaims his handiwork.
> Day pours out the word to day,
>   and night to night imparts knowledge;
> Not a word nor a discourse
>   whose voice is not heard;
> Through all the earth their voice resounds,
>   and to the ends of the world, their message.

---

[5] The order in this part of the paper is theological rather than historical. It is clear that Israel became aware of Yahweh as her national God before she understood him to be Lord and Creator of all things. The historical order is followed more closely in E. Beaucamp, O.F.M., *The Bible and the Universe*, London 1963, which has many observations which are relevant to this paper.

[6] Cf. *Gen.* 14:19 and 23.

[7] Cf. *Ps.* 135.

He has pitched a tent there for the sun,
  which comes forth like the groom from his bridal chamber
  and, like a giant, joyfully runs its course.
At one end of the heavens it comes forth,
  and its course is to their other end;
  nothing escapes its heat.

Ps. 18:2-7a.

This message of Yahweh's glory is—one might say—preached with such insistence by creation that men can hardly resist his claims:

The heavens proclaim his justice,
  and all peoples see his glory.

All who worship graven things are put to shame,
  who glory in the things of nought;
  all gods are prostrate before him.

Ps. 96:6-7.

No song of praise is complete which does not invite the whole of creation to join in. Whether it is an individual Israelite or the whole nation or even the whole of mankind that wishes to praise the great goodness of Yahweh, the harmony is imperfect unless completed by the full chorus of creation:

Praise Yahweh from the heavens,
  praise him in the heights;
Praise him, all you his angels
  praise him, all you his hosts.
Praise him, sun and moon;
  praise him, all you shining stars.
Praise him, you highest heavens,
  and you waters above the heavens.
Let them praise the name of Yahweh,
  for he commanded and they were created;
He established them forever and ever;
  he gave them a duty which shall not pass away.

Ps. 148:1-6[8].

---

[8] Cf. also *Pss.* 88:6-10; 95:1-9 etc., and the Benedicite chant from *Daniel* 3:57-88 which priests recite after Mass.

The whole of creation reacts to the tone of God's interventions; creatures rejoice at his saving activity:

> Let the heavens and the earth praise him,
>   and seas and whatever moves in them!

> For God will save Sion
>   and rebuild the cities of Juda.
>
> *Ps.* 68:35-36a (cf. 65:1).

but they tremble when he comes in judgment:

> You are terrible; and who can withstand you
>   for the fury of your anger?
> From heaven you made your intervention heard;
>   the earth feared and was silent
> When God arose for judgment,
>   to save all the afflicted of the earth.
>
> *Ps.* 75:8-10.

> The waters saw you, O God;
>   the waters saw you and shuddered;
>   the very depths were troubled.
>
> *Ps.* 76:17.

Creatures depend on their Creator for their every need. Having described how God provides for the needs and the nourishment of man and beast, the author of Psalm 103 sums up his thoughts:

> They all look to you
>   to give them food in due time.
> When you give it to them, they gather it;
>   when you open your hand, they are filled with good things.
> If you hide your face, they are dismayed;
>   if you take away their breath, they perish
>   and return to their dust.
> When you send forth your spirit, they are created,
>   and you renew the face of the earth.
>
> *Ps.* 103:27-30.

It is because God is the God of heaven and earth that he can do what he likes in heaven and earth:

> For I know that Yahweh is great;
>   our Lord is greater than all gods.
> All that Yahweh wills he does
>   in heaven and on earth,
>   in the seas and in all the deeps.
> He raises storm clouds from the end of the earth;
>   with the lightning he makes the rain;
>   he brings forth the winds from his storehouse.
>
> *Ps.* 134:5-7.

This God is all-powerful but his power is wisely applied since he is everywhere present and fully aware of every occurrence which demands his intervention whether to judge or to save:

> Understand, you senseless ones among the people;
>   and, you fools, when will you be wise?
> Shall he who shaped the ear not hear?
>   or he who formed the eye not see?
> Shall he who instructs nations not chastise,
>   he who teaches men knowledge?
> Yahweh knows the thoughts of men,
>   and that they are vain.
>
> *Ps.* 93:8-11.

None can escape his judgment, if he has sinned:

> Where can I go from your spirit?
>   from your presence where can I flee?
> If I go up to the heavens, you are there;
>   if I sink to the nether world, you are present there.
> If I take the wings of the dawn,
>   if I settle at the farthest limits of the sea,
> Even there your hand shall guide me,
>   and your right hand hold me fast.
> If I say, "Surely the darkness shall hide me,
>   and night shall be my light"—
> For you darkness itself is not dark,
>   and night shines as the day.
>
> *Ps.* 138:7-12.

But the one who has the Lord on his side is happy, and he can best secure his protection by a blameless life:[9]

> Happy he whose help is the God of Jacob,
>   whose hope is in Yahweh, his God,
> Who made heaven and earth,
>   the sea and all that is in them;
> Who keeps faith forever,
>   secures justice for the oppressed,
>   gives food to the hungry.

Ps. 145:5-7.

> Were I to cherish wickedness in my heart,
>   Yahweh would not hear;
> But God has heard;
>   he has hearkened to the sound of my prayer.

Ps. 65:18-19.

As the Lord of creation, Yahweh has at his disposal the creatures of the world when he wishes to save and to rescue:

> Fire goes before him
>   and consumes his foes round about.

Ps. 96:3.

> Bless Yahweh, O my soul!
>   O Yahweh, my God, you are great indeed!
> You are clothed with majesty and glory,
>   robed in light as with a cloak.
> You have spread out the heavens like a tent-cloth;
>   you have constructed your palace upon the waters.
> You make the clouds your chariot;
>   you travel on the wings of the wind.
> You make the winds your messengers,
>   and flaming fire your ministers.

Ps. 103:1-4.[10]

This brief examination of the relationship between the Creator and creatures as seen by the Israelite writers showed their con-

---

[9] This insistence on moral conduct is repeated at every stage of biblical revelation from God's command to Adam and Eve to his words to Abraham: "Walk before me and be perfect" (*Gen.* 17:1), from the ten commandments to the Sermon on the Mount.

[10] Cf. *Isaiah* 40:12.

tinual awareness of the dependence of all things on God. But
this was not something they grasped like a metaphysical principle,
but something which they perceived in the life and movement of
every being around them. The regular pattern of their movements
and their instinctive behaviour[11] spoke to them of the wisdom of
their Creator. Indeed, this wisdom was such an obvious characteristic of God's creation that Hebrew writers personified it and
set it in his presence like a master workman while God was
creating.[12]

The antiphonal psalm 135 with its frequently-repeated "*quoniam
in aeternum misericordia ejus*" is also instructive in this context. It
is an acclaim which greets not only God's saving activity in
Israel's history but every work of his creation (cf. vv. 1-9).
Creation is as much a work of God's goodness, mercy, love,
loving kindness—depending on how one translates the Hebrew
hesed—as is his devotedness to his chosen people.

The exposition so far has dealt with what one may call the
metaphysical or theological relationship between God and all
creatures. In the course of history this relationship was refined
by a special intervention of God as a result of which he bound
the people of Israel to himself by a special bond. No longer was
there question so much of the God who was the Creator of the
heavens and the earth as the God of Abraham, Isaac and Jacob,
the God of Israel. It is true that the God of the patriarchs was
also the God who was the Creator of heaven and earth, but the
title "God of Israel" expressed a relationship which was more
intimate and more personal as a result of God's own choice.

When making this special agreement with his chosen people,
God revealed himself under the name of Yahweh. Most people
who read the Bible in translation lose the significance of this
proper name. The derivation of the word is uncertain but it
most likely comes from the verb "to be" or the verb "to become"[13]
and when used in the context of the alliance with Israel it draws

[11] *Ps.* 103:5-30.
[12] Cf. *Prov.* 8:22 ff.
[13] Zorrell in *Lexicon Hebraicum et Aramaicum Veteris Testamenti*, Rome
1956, s.v. renders the name "is qui est". Albright regards it as causative: "he
causes to be", cf. W. F. Albright, *From the Stone Age to Christianity*, New
York 1957, 56-7. Kohler on the other hand in his *Lexicon in VT libros* s.v.
describes the word as a noun meaning "being or existence".

attention to the fact that the God who is the Creator of all things establishes an intimate relationship with one alone of all the peoples on the face of the earth. Over the centuries Yahweh built up for himself a record of unfailing care for Israel and unbroken fidelity to his promises. The proper name Yahweh when used instead of the common name "God" recalled the special bond which linked him with Israel and evoked the memory of his frequent interventions in history on her behalf.

The use of the name Jesus in New Testament revelation offers a parallel. It is true that Jesus is God, but the name Jesus has rather different implications from the word God. The holy name Jesus includes by implication the whole work of the Incarnation and Redemption which involved an intervention in the history of the world resembling the interventions of Yahweh in the Old Testament era. And just as we love God with a particular affection when we think of him in terms of Jesus and the benefits we have derived from the Incarnation, so the Israelites loved God with a special affection when they thought of him as Yahweh, the Father of his people, who intervenes in history to rescue and to save.

The awareness of this use of the proper name of the God of the covenant is lost in most translations because, following the Septuagint, "Lord" is generally read instead of Yahweh. While this usage emphasizes that the God of Israel is the God of all mankind, it has the disadvantage of obscuring the gradual revelation of himself through the centuries. It also tends to hide the growth in love which urged him to act with increasing generosity towards Israel, a generosity which culminated in the giving of himself in the Incarnation.[14]

The Bible conceives of this relationship between Yahweh and Israel as established by a covenant or agreement in which the prime mover is Yahweh himself.[15] Through this covenant he selects a small group of people from all the races of the earth to be his own in a special way. The simplest form of the covenant

---

[14] This consideration of the name Yahweh is relevant to an understanding of the sacraments of the New Law as encounters with Christ. They run parallel to Israel's encounters with Yahweh in the saving events of her history.

[15] The supreme liberty of God's choice of Israel—and of his bestowal of grace—is described in *Ezekiel* 16, one of the most moving passages in the whole Bible.

can be stated: "I shall be your God and you shall be my people".[16]
As a result of this covenant Yahweh-God, the Creator of the
heavens and the earth, becomes father of his chosen people with
the obligation of exercising a father's loving care in its regard.[17]
They, in their turn, must respond by the devoted obedience of a
loving child.[18] To ensure the welfare of his family, the God of
Israel has at his disposal all the powers which were his as Creator
of the heavens and the earth and the history of his chosen people
shows him exercising them to rescue and to protect as well as to
chastise and develop his often wayward child.

The saving activity of God the Creator on behalf of his own
people is emphasized in some of the Psalms.[19] They portray
poetically, and with the freedom which poetry allows, the epic
struggle of Yahweh the Creator with the Egyptian king. God's
creatures did his bidding to bring the Pharaoh to his knees. Life-
giving water was turned into nauseating blood; light was ex-
tinguished by darkness and myriads of insects and pests brought
famine and disease to a rebellious people. It was useless for
Pharaoh to persist in the unequal struggle with the Creator of all
things who now applied his power on behalf of his beloved Israel.
If Pharaoh weakened under the loss of the first-born, he foolishly
re-entered the lists and met disaster when the waters opened to
let Israel pass and closed to engulf his army.

In the desert the rocks gushed living water at Yahweh's command and quails and manna in abundance gave miraculous relief
to a people on the verge of starvation. It was surely the function
of God, their Father, to see that Israel had food and drink—not
only to survive, but to have the strength to reach their goal.
Yahweh was so conscious of what one might call his self-imposed
duty that he used his omnipotent control of creatures to ensure
its fulfilment. Such measures were necessary in view of the special
destiny of Israel and were marks of the affection borne to her
by her loving Spouse.

This Exodus event is of prime importance in the history of

---

[16] *Lev.* 26:12.
[17] *Deut.* 32:6.
[18] *Exod.* 24:7.
[19] Cf. *Pss.* 77, 104, 105, 135 and the book of Exodus for this and succeeding
paragraphs.

Israel. It was the occasion on which Yahweh made Israel his chosen son, or to use another metaphor, the occasion of his espousals with Israel. Either metaphor emphasizes the part which love played in this relationship. The terms of the covenant which gave lasting and legal form to this alliance between God and his people opens with a command to love: Thou shalt love the Lord thy God.[20] In fulfilling this command Israel was only responding to the love which Yahweh had lavished on her.[21]

It was not a love, however, which she always found it easy to give for many other rivals competed with Yahweh for her hand. The fleeting attractions of an unlawful alliance with a Canaanite god often bewitched her and made her forget the terms of her relationship with Yahweh.[22] It was therefore essential to keep before her the memory of Yahweh's saving acts in ritual, story and song, so that the recollection of his generosity in the past as well as the consciousness of his present help would support her in time of temptation. With Yahweh's help she could live a life worthy of one who had, as it were, been taken into the family of God.

The Israelites needed particularly to recall the great events of the Exodus. This was done in connection with the celebration of the Passover feast which included the sacrifice of the Paschal Lamb, the eating of unleavened bread and bitter herbs, and the carrying out of these now-sacred rites with staff in hand and shod for a journey. In the celebration of this feast we can see how long years after the Exodus had taken place material things were used to capture the graces of that great gesture of God's love. In themselves, the actions performed were not necessarily significant from a religious point of view. They required to be set in a particular context so that the doing of them should speak its message and produce its effect. Their mysterious character required an explanation, especially for those who had never before witnessed them. For this reason the instructions of God concerning the celebration of the paschal meal include the following item: "When your children say to you: 'What do you mean by this service?', you shall say it is the sacrifice of the Lord's Passover,

[20] *Deut.* 6:5.
[21] Cf. *Osee* 1-3.
[22] Cf. *Jerem.* 3.

for he passed over the houses of the people of Israel in Egypt
when he slew the Egyptians but spared our houses".[23]

This is but a brief formula which indicates in the broadest
possible way the context which gives meaning to the actions of
the Israelites who celebrated the Passover. But the Old Testament
itself shows that in practice a lengthy exposition of the salvation
event accompanied the ritual. The book of *Exodus* has drawn
on several such accounts of the struggle between Pharaoh and
Yahweh, the God of Israel and the Creator of the world, to give
us its present narrative.[24]

Yahweh makes full use of his created instruments and scourges
Egypt into submission with the plagues, while delivering his
people by a miraculous path through the waters. When they had
escaped from the threat of the Egyptian army, the Israelites
believed themselves faced with an even worse fate, death in the
desert by thirst and starvation. But just as God the Creator gives
food to his creatures in due time so that they may live, Yahweh
the God of Israel provides her with the requisite nourishment so
that she may reach her promised destination.

Numerous psalms also show how these events were recalled in
songs of triumph and hymns of praise which were undoubtedly
sung in the course of the ritual.[25]

These narratives and hymns gave point and meaning to what
the Israelites were doing when they celebrated the ritual of the
paschal feast. Yahweh who did these things in the past was
Yahweh the Creator intervening with power on behalf of his
people. Although Israel may have been unfaithful, Yahweh is
unchanged. He still loves his chosen people and is still willing
to exercise his full power on her behalf. With his infinite awareness
of her needs, he is ready to help her even now—as he will always
be ready to help her—if only she would call on him, if only she
would keep faith with her spouse. With his help, no matter how

---

[23] *Exod.* 12:26-7.
[24] Recent study of the Pentateuch has shown that the various traditions
which combine to give us our present text developed in conjunction with
the celebration of the great religious festivals at the Israelite sanctuaries. Cf.
de Vaux, *La Genèse*, Paris 1953, 18-19; Robert-Feuillet, *Introduction à la
Bible*, I, 278 ff.
[25] Cf. the Hallel (*Pss.* 112-117) which was sung during the paschal feast
and also *Pss.* 77, 104, 105, 135 etc.

great the obstacles may seem, no matter how disabling her weakness, she could still reach the Promised Land. The repetition of this ritual speaks for itself once set in its proper context, but the dramatic re-telling of these ancient stories with all the artifice of poetry and literature makes their impact even greater.

The ritual of the Exodus includes an injunction to repeat this rite in succeeding generations: "You shall observe this rite as an ordinance for you and for your sons for ever, and when you come to the land which the Lord will give you as he has promised you shall keep this service".[26] If this rite is repeated, so also is its explanation as is clear from the variety of treatment it receives in the Old Testament. One can best emphasize the importance of the history of Israel—salvation history—for the understanding of these rites and ultimately for their fruitfulness by reference to Psalm 77:1-8:

1   Hearken, my people, to my teaching;
        incline your ears to the words of my mouth.
2   I will open my mouth in a parable,
        I will utter mysteries from of old.
3   What we have heard and know,
        and what our fathers have declared to us,
4   We will not hide from their sons;
        we will declare to the generation to come
        The glorious deeds of Yahweh and his strength
        and the wonders that he wrought.
5   He set it up as a decree in Jacob,
        and established it as a law in Israel,
        That what he commanded our fathers
        they should make known to their sons;
6   So that the generation to come might know,
        their sons yet to be born,
        That they too may rise and declare to their sons
7   that they should put their hope in God,
        And not forget the deeds of God
        but keep his commands,

[26] *Exod.* 12:24-5.

8   And not be like their fathers,
        a generation wayward and rebellious,
     A generation that kept not its heart steadfast
        nor its spirit faithful toward God.

This psalm outlines what one could call a theology of history, and the opening verses introduce a fairly detailed poetic account of the history of Israel. They refer first of all to the fact that this history of Israel is the gradual revelation of the mystery of God, a theme which St Paul was later to develop. Israel's relation to Yahweh was indeed a mystery, a riddle[27] whose solution in terms of God's love was gradually unfolded in her history (cf. vv. 1-2).

In order that continuity might be maintained and that every generation should have, as it were, the whole story, the account of Yahweh's glorious deeds in each generation must be passed on to the next (cf. v. 4). They in their turn must do the same for the generations to come. There should be no break in the tradition which was to give every generation of Israel hope for the future (cf. v. 7) and an unfailing expectation of the final fulfilment of God's plans. Their participation in Yahweh's final triumph would necessarily involve fidelity to the covenant through the observance of his commands (cf. vv. 5 and 7-8).

This all-too-brief outline of some important institutions and events of the Old Testament draws attention to certain aspects of the sacraments which are often neglected through excessive concentration on efficient causality. The material, final, and formal causes of the sacraments also deserve consideration especially for the contribution they can make to the meaning of the sacraments.

Meaning is directed to man's intellect, one of the spiritual faculties of man and—in so far as the spiritual faculties enjoy a primacy—those aspects of the sacraments which are meant to receive its attention should not be neglected. Indeed, the complete neglect of these aspects would reduce the use of the sacraments almost to the level of superstitious practice. The prophets of Israel castigated those Jews who offered sacrifice without regard for the meaning of what they did. Their actions both before and

[27] The Hebrew word translated by "mysteries" in v. 2b above also means "riddles".

after the offering of the sacrifice showed a complete disregard for the wishes of God, and their sacrifice could never be regarded as an act of worship. They did not put their minds to what they were doing, their heart was not in their offering, and what resulted was not so much an expression of religion as an act of hypocrisy or even of superstition. The Old Testament insists that the meaning of ritual must be grasped if the rite is to be truly expressive of the religious attitude of the worshipper and beneficial for his soul.[28] This obviously has relevance for the New Testament sacraments, which, although peculiarly effective rites, still belong to the category of ritual and are subject to its laws.[29]

The Old Testament sets the materials chosen as God's saving instruments in the wider context of material creation as a whole, which God saw was good, and which constantly sings his praises in song without words; words in fact are not necessary for each being speaks a message simply by being what it is and by following out the law of its nature.

When particular items of the material creation are adopted by God for sacramental use they are transferred to a new context in which they speak even more eloquently the goodness of the Creator as manifested to his chosen people.[30] The fundamental relation of these creatures to the Creator should never be forgotten, because it is the basis for the practice of recollection in a sacramental spirituality. If, for example, water is chosen by God as the means for communicating new life in the sacrament of baptism, frequent experience of our dependence on water should remind us of the life we have received with its help, not to mention the occasions when Yahweh made use of it to produce and preserve life. If bread is the form under which our sacramental food is given to us, this stupendous use of our staple food must surely give us a new reverence for it. Those who make use of this gift which God gives to gladden the heart of man[31] should

---

[28] Cf. *Isaiah* 1:10-17; *Amos* 5:21 ff.; *Ps.* 49:7 ff.
[29] Cf. L. Bouyer, *Le rite et l'homme*, Paris 1962. (E. tr. *Rite and Man*, London, 1963).
[30] These remarks are concerned with the material cause of the sacraments. Usually the matter of the sacraments is considered in so far as it is part of the efficient cause without much reference to the broader context to which this "matter" belongs, and which is outlined here.
[31] Cf. *Ps.* 103:15.

remember that through this creature of God they receive the graces of the Eucharist. The materials used in the sacraments therefore speak to us of Jesus Christ, our Redeemer, but they also show forth the glory of the Creator and present the work of the Incarnation as the restoration of all things—even material things—in Christ.[32]

It has been mentioned in the previous paragraph that the use of God's creatures in the context of salvation gave them a significantly new meaning. This was brought out especially by the words which accompanied their use, as was shown in the case of the paschal supper.[33] Creatures speak the glory of their Creator; the events of the Exodus spoke the love of Yahweh for Israel to those who experienced them. The ritual of the paschal meal repeats this story of love to generations of the faithful. Such material actions divorced from words are symbolic actions and it can be said with some truth that the benefit or meaning one derives from such symbolic actions is proportioned to what one puts into them.

It is here that the words which accompany the ritual of the Old Testament and sacramental symbols of the New are of greatest assistance. The formula supplied by the ritual may be extremely brief as was the formula for the paschal meal, but it is intended merely as a summary of what has been learned elsewhere,

---

[32] Cf. *Col.* 1:20. The prophets describe in lyrical terms the blessedness in which the material world will share when it is freed from subjection to sinful man and when God's dominion will be finally and perfectly realized. Cf. e.g *Isaiah* 11:6 ff.; 65:17; 66:22; *Amos* 9:13. The Apocalypse speaks of "a new heaven and a new earth" (21:1 ff.) which are inaugurated through the saving activity of the Lamb. In the sacraments of the New Law material things are empowered to produce effects which properly speaking belong to the era of the new heaven and the new earth. This power which derives from Christ contributes not only to the salvation of man but also hastens the deliverance of material creation which groans as it awaits liberation (*Rom.* 8:19 ff.).

[33] What is said here is intended to stress the importance of the meaning of the words which are spoken during the administration of the sacraments. These words I refer to will obviously include what we call the "form" of the sacrament, but must not be limited to those words alone. The accompanying prayers, addresses etc. are extremely important for the meaningful reception of the sacraments. Generally the words of the form are considered more in relation to efficiency—as part of the efficient cause—rather than under the heading of meaning, and while they are referred to as the form of the sacrament they do not receive the consideration which the formal cause of the sacraments should get.

a phrase or two to jog the memory of the recipient.[34] He is reminded that this rite is a summing up of thousands of years of
salvation history, a concentration of the saving power and loving
care of God, Creator and Redeemer, on his person. This power
and care are applied to him in the way which best fits his needs
in accordance with the grace proper to each sacrament.

A striking feature of Israel's history is her continual pre-
occupation with the future, or perhaps one should say with her
future.[35] From the first promise made to Abraham which included
the Promised Land and his being a source of blessing to all
nations, Israel was aware that she was the chosen instrument of
God for the realization of his plans for man, and, indeed, for
the whole world, since the blessedness of other nations and the
prosperity of the material world was mysteriously linked with the
triumph of God's own people.

Every event of history whether it brought prosperity or disaster
to Israel in some way promoted the designs of God. Slavery in
Egypt was necessary that the Exodus might take place. This was
the first act of rescue experienced by Israel as a people and in the
course of it she was bound to Yahweh in a covenant of love. If
Yahweh brought her out of Egypt, it was to bring her to the
Promised Land. If he fed her with manna in the desert and drew
water from the rocks, it was to give her the strength to get there.
This great act of rescue became normative for the future of
Israel and subsequent events were thought of in terms of the
Exodus. If Israel was brought into captivity in Babylon, it was
in order that she might be brought back to the Promised Land

[34] This is particularly true of the formula for baptism which sums up the
teaching received by the catechumen during the Lenten season.

[35] The paragraphs which follow consider the sacraments in relation to their
final cause. The Eucharist is sometimes described as the "finis omnium sacramentorum" (St Thomas, *S. theol.* III, 63, 6c and 65, 3c), but is itself, like the
other sacraments, a means towards achieving unity with God which will
be perfected only in the new Promised Land. It is instructive to consider the
sacramental system of the New Testament in relation to our final destiny
expressed in terms of a new exodus and a new entry into a promised land,
but the paragraphs which follow can only give the barest outline of how this
might be done. When theologians say that the Eucharist is the *finis omnium
sacramentorum* they are considering how the sacraments are related to one
another within the sacramental system. The exodus context, however, not
only relates the sacraments to one another but also clarifies the ultimate
purpose of the whole sacramental system.

by an exodus accompanied by even greater signs than the Exodus
from Egypt. The desert would again run with water when Yahweh
would lead his people from Babylon as he had led them from
Egypt in the cloud.[36]

When ritual was used to recall these events, it too contributed
to the advance of Israel towards her goal. The recollection of past
events reminded her that Yahweh who had intervened on previous
occasions was a living God. The power he had exercised in the
past was still available to Israel, and would always be available
to ensure that she would realize the divine plan. Such thoughts
equipped Israel with hope and strength to face the demands of
her vocation.

It is not surprising that the Christian Church becoming aware
of itself as the people of God adopted these ideas and pictured its
destiny in terms of the Exodus and the journey towards the
Promised Land.[37] These Exodus themes occur throughout the
New Testament, and are particularly prominent in the Apocalypse.[38]

When seen in this Exodus context, the sacraments of the New
Law are more clearly related to their ultimate purpose. The
Church moves through a history which is under the control of
the Lamb, the Lord of history, towards its share in the triumph
of the Lamb.

Baptism, like circumcision, makes one a member of the People
of God and gives one a right to an inheritance in the Promised
Land.[39] It reminds one of how Israel became the chosen people
by passing through the waters of the Red Sea and entered into
its inheritance through the waters of the Jordan. The Creator who
brought life from the waters of the great deep at the beginning
of creation recreates us through the waters of baptism so that

[36] *Isaiah* 40:3 ff.; 41:17 ff.; 43:16 ff.
[37] Cf. *Hebrews* 3:7 ff.; *Matt.* 5:4. Some see a reference to this exodus theme
in the use of the word exodus for Christ's death in *Luke* 9:31. In any event,
by dying on the occasion of the paschal feast, Christ set his work of redemption
in a paschal and exodus context in which the early Church clearly saw him
as the new paschal lamb (*John* 1:36; 19:36; 1 *Peter* 1:19; *Apoc. passim*).
[38] *Apoc.* 5:6-10; 11:14-19; 14:1-5; 15:2-4 etc.
[39] *Gal.* 3:26 ff.; *Rom.* 6:1 ff.; 8:14 ff.

re-born and regenerated we begin to live the life of the sons of God.[40]

Confirmation gives the gift of the Spirit which inspired the prophets and leaders of old and equipped them for their leadership of Israel.[41] For the messianic times, the times of the Church, a more abundant outpouring of the Spirit was promised and all would be equipped with its power for the more effective realization of God's grand designs.[42]

The Eucharist is the manna which came down from heaven and gives eternal life, the life which is characteristic of the new Promised Land. Those who sit at the Eucharistic table partake of a food which has been prepared for them in the sacrifice of the Eucharist, which is the covenant sacrifice, a renewal of the agreement made on our behalf and in our name by Christ and sealed in his precious blood. All these elements are foreshadowed in the making of the Old Covenant at Mount Sinai, in the sealing of the agreement with blood and in the custom of eating a sacrificial meal when the victim had been offered.

Penance is the purification from sin which by disposing of the obstacles which prevent one's return to God make possible a renewal of the covenant through the Eucharistic sacrifice. Whenever Israel fell away in her service of Yahweh, the seal was set on her return and she could begin afresh when she had renewed the covenant with her Lord and promised fidelity for the future. A pre-requisite for this renewal of the covenant was a suitable acknowledgment of her guilt.[43] St Paul insists on just such a preparation for the reception of the Eucharist principally because of the real presence of Christ in the Eucharist. It is, however, possible that this reference to the "cup of the new covenant in my blood"[44] may hint at the insincerity in associating oneself publicly with the covenant and the New Law of Christ while failing to carry out its basic precept of love.

---

[40] The readings in the Easter vigil liturgy focus attention on these aspects of the sacrament.

[41] Cf. *Num.* 11:24; 27:18; *Judges* 6:34; *Ezech.* 37:1 etc.

[42] *Isaiah* 11:2 ff.; 59:21; *Joel* 2:28 ff. and the dominant role of the Spirit under the New Law, cf. e.g. 2 *Cor.* 3:6-18; *Acts passim.*

[43] Cf. *Joshua* 24:14 ff.; *Ezra* 6:21; 9-10:1-17; 2 *Chron.* 29:3-30:27; 2 *Chron.* 34 and 35; *Isaiah* 53:6; *Ps.* 50:6.

[44] 1 *Cor.* 11:25.

In so far as extreme unction shares with penance the function of forgiving sin, it prepares for the worthy renewal of the covenant and an abundant sharing in its blessing, but the rite of anointing which is proper to this sacrament is rich in symbolism. An abundance of oil was among the many attractions of the Promised Land,[45] and it became part of the staple diet of the Israelites.[46] It symbolized prosperity,[47] joy[48] and good health,[49] and was even used for healing wounds.[50]

The injunction to anoint the sick with oil in the Name (of the Lord) correlates this symbolism with the saving power of the name of Jesus. This is primarily a work of redemption from sin and therefore of spiritual healing, a clearly-declared effect of the sacrament: "if he has committed sins, he will be forgiven".[51] It often happens that the sick person is not restored to health by this sacrament and since good health is thus frequently divorced from the symbol of good health, one may perhaps look beyond the immediate condition of the body to the radiant health it will enjoy in the Promised Land, "where death shall be no more, nor shall there be mourning, nor crying nor pain".[52]

Holy orders recalls the position of Aaron, anointed priest[53] and leader of the cult offered by a priestly nation.[54] The people of Israel gathered round their high priest as he offered sacrifice foreshadowed the members of the Church at the altar of Christ participating in the priestly offering through the sacramental character. This too is a preparation for the heavenly liturgy described in the Apocalypse.[55]

The natural institution of marriage was a worthy symbol of the union between Yahweh and Israel, his spouse. To tell the story of Israel's fitful response to Yahweh's faithful love is to

[45] *Deut.* 32:13-14; *Osee* 2:5-8; *Ezech.* 16:13.
[46] *Ecclus.* 39:31 (or 26).
[47] *Ps.* 2:5; *Eccles.* 9:8.
[48] *Ps.* 44:8.
[49] *Ps.* 103:14-15.
[50] *Isaiah* 1:6; *Luke* 10:34.
[51] *James* 5:15.
[52] *Apoc.* 21:4. Cf. also *Heb.* 1:8-9 where "oil of gladness" is used to describe the happiness of Christ in glory. Cf. C. Spicq, *L'Épître aux Hébreux*, II, Paris 1953, 19.
[53] *Exodus* 29:7.
[54] *Exodus* 19:6.
[55] *Apoc.* 4:9-11; 7:15-17; 20:6; 1 *Peter* 2:9.

enrich the concept of Christian marriage which in turn represents the union between Christ and his Church. It is in terms of this sacrament that the author of the Apocalypse depicts the final act of God's drama of salvation when he sees the Lamb united in glory to his bride, the holy city, the heavenly Jerusalem.[56]

Readers of the Old Testament have often noticed the pre-occupation of many of the writers with the people as a whole, with the community, rather than with the individual. One might say too that the interventions of Yahweh in the Exodus event were aimed at rescuing the people as a whole and establishing them in their new home as a group. While this is a thought which requires refinement and qualification there is sufficient truth in it to invite us to attend to the "social" aspects of the sacraments. We receive them not merely as individuals to sanctify our souls but also as members of the People of God to extend his kingship throughout creation. Not only do we draw nearer to the Promised Land by their reception; we also add a stone to the building of the heavenly Jerusalem, and prepare a home not for ourselves alone but for all who are invited to the marriage of the Lamb.

Each of these themes could be the object of a separate study, but it is hoped that the brief mention of them in this context may draw attention to the ordering of the sacraments towards our final destiny. The Old Testament therefore with its less efficient "sacraments"—if one may put it that way—can contribute greatly to our understanding of the sacraments of the New Law.[57]

---

[56] Cf. *Osee* 1-3; *Ezechiel* 16; *Ephesians* 5:21-33; *Apoc.* 21 and 22.
[57] I have confined myself almost exclusively to the Old Testament in this paper. Those who wish to read how the Fathers used Old Testament themes when considering the sacraments may turn to books like: P. Palmer, *Sources of Christian Theology, Sacraments and Forgiveness*, London 1959; J. Danielou, *The Bible and the Liturgy*, London 1960.

Christ, Sacrament of God

DENIS O'CALLAGHAN

IN a collection of papers on the sacraments a paper on "Christ, Sacrament of God" may seem at first sight somewhat distant from the main theme. But the relevance of the subject would not be questioned by the Christians of St Paul's day nor by the Fathers. For them Christianity or the Christian mystery was Christ; he was at once the gift of God's love to men extending into and active in every communication of the divine life and at the same time the only way by which men could go to the Father, the ultimate term and source of all life and love. The evolution of scientific theology atomized this simple vision into distinct departments, each dealing with a given aspect. Inevitably the effort to explain each doctrine, action, sacrament, within its own terms involved a specification which hampered the total vision. In particular, sacramental theology occupied itself with the individual signs, with the nature of their causality, with their *ex opere operato* efficacy, with the minister, subject and effects— Christ and the redemption was the affair of Christology.

Modern theology enjoys the benefit of the detailed working out of the specific aspects over the centuries, but it strives to deepen its understanding and to achieve again a global view of our faith by placing everything in a single perspective reaching back through Christ to the Father.

Fundamentally Christianity is a mystery—the self-gift of the absolutely transcendent God communicating himself to men through Christ so that man in the encounter with Christ can enter into a personal friendship with God. There are three levels in this mystery. Firstly, the mystery of God considered in himself, infinitely distant, holy, unapproachable but yet the source of all life and love. Secondly, the mystery of Christ, which is the marvellous expression of God's love in time; the Son has become flesh to bring God to men and men to God. Thirdly, the mystery of the Church in faith and sacrament, where the incarnate Word and his saving acts continue present so that men may go to the Father through him.

This vision of Christianity-Mystery of Christ owes a great deal to Dom Odo Casel.[1] Disagree as one will with his doctrine of the *Mysteriengegenwart*—the actual mode of presence of Christ and his redemption in the liturgy—one cannot deny that his basic intuition has the simplicity of truth and has had untold influence on present-day theological and liturgical thought.

The phrase "mystery of Christ" favoured by Casel emphasizes the *content* of the salvation-economy, the divine life and love which is there contained and offered to men. The phrase "Christ —sacrament of God" underlines the *mode* of this mystery, the manner of God's love-gift of himself to man—the divine life is offered to us by a *visible* intervention of God into time and history which signifies his will and readiness to save man and which actually *contains* that salvation. Christ in his human nature is the primordial or foundation sacrament; in him God invades time to bring man into supernatural union with himself. The constitution and sanctification of God's people by word or sacrament is to be seen in function of Christ. The Dutch theologian Schillebeeckx[2] has been particularly associated with the appreciation of Christ as the sacrament of God, and the notion

[1] See O. Casel, *The Mystery of Christian Worship and Other Writings*, London 1962, 5-7, *et passim*.

[2] E. H. Schillebeeckx, *Le Christ, sacrament de la rencontre de Dieu*, Paris 1960. Sheed and Ward have published an English version of this important work—*Christ, The Sacrament of Encounter with God*. The main themes have been repeated in "The Sacraments: an Encounter with God", *Christianity Divided* (edited by Oberman-O'Hanlon-Callahan), London 1962, 245-275.

has been incorporated in the schema on the liturgy recently approved in draft by the ecumenical council.

The terms "mystery-sacrament" demand a few words of explanation. *Mysterion* was widely used in the Greek world of St. Paul's day with some variety of meaning, pivoting on its basic derivation of secrecy (μύειν τὸ στομά)—a confided secret, a secret doctrine, symbol. In the mystery-religions it was employed (chiefly in the plural *mysteria*) to indicate the secret cults to which the initiated alone had access. In the Greek text of the Synoptics (*Matt.* 13:11; *Mark* 4:11; *Luke* 8:10) it occurs in the phrase "the mysteries of the kingdom of heaven", which are manifested only to the disciples. These are the hidden elements and truths which constitute the nature of the kingdom which Christ had come to establish. This concept is familiar to us from the Septuagint—in *Tobias* 12:7 and *Judith* 2:2 the mystery is the secret decision which the king or leader communicates only to those in his confidence. The Aramaic term used by Christ for mystery is not known to us, but in the Synoptics it is rendered *musterion*, and so in Matthew and Mark we have an instance of the use of the word even prior to its employment by St Paul.

In rendering the Pauline *musterion* St Jerome uses indiscriminately the Latin *mysterium* (*Rom.* 11:25, *Col.* 1:26—"Mysterium quod absconditum fuit a saeculis") and *sacramentum* (*Eph.* 1:9, 3:3, 3:9—"Sacramenti absconditi"). The writings of the Fathers also employ *mysterium* and *sacramentum* as synonyms.

The introduction of the term *sacramentum* to translate *mysterium* is in itself something of a mystery. There is little basis in the classical meanings of the word to sustain the usage. In classical Latin it is used in two senses only—firstly, of the oath taken by the Roman soldiers to their *imperator*, and hence of any oath; secondly, of the pledge or security deposited in public keeping by the parties in a lawsuit, and hence of a lawsuit in general. Both meanings, especially the former, contributed something to the Christian usage but they do not explain it. Christine Mohrmann[3] thinks that the word *mysterium* was discarded by the western Church because of its connection with the mystery-religions, and it is suggested that from an early date the word

[3] *Latin vulgaire, latin des chrétiens*, Paris 1952, 31.

sacramentum was employed in popular parlance to translate mystery, a meaning suggested by its derivation (*sacer*) but which has left no trace in extant literature apart from Christian writers.[4] (This popular meaning may well be unintentionally preserved in Pliny's account of the Christian way of life in his letter to the Emperor Trajan, *Epistle* 96).

In the early Church mystery and sacrament had a much wider meaning than that current in later centuries. For us mystery has come to mean chiefly a truth or doctrine which human reason cannot comprehend, and from the time of Peter Lombard sacrament has been almost exclusively employed to connote the seven liturgical rites which confer grace *ex opere operato*. The original usage of mystery-sacrament was much more flexible[5]—it was applied not only to the Mass, the seven sacraments, and various liturgical acts, but to Christian doctrine, Church discipline and the whole Christian religion. In particular, it was used to denote the divine plan of salvation, and the mysteries of Christ's life (*sacramentum passionis, incarnationis, paschatis*)—here sacrament means a truth or incident which has hidden divine salvific meaning and content. It was in this sense of sacrament-mystery that the Fathers would interpret the phrase "Christ, sacrament of God"—"*Non est enim aliud Dei sacramentum nisi Christus*", says St Augustine.[6] The modern use brings to the surface the theological nuances of the phrase—it indicates Christ as the *Ursakrament*, the visible sign of God's love and involvement with men. Christ is the visible divine intervention in human history signifying God's will to give the grace of salvation and actually bestowing that saving grace. To understand this as an analogy or figure of speech borrowed from the department of sacramental theology would indicate topsy-turvy thinking. Our seven sacraments are sacraments only because they are extensions of the sacramentality of Christ.

It goes without saying that this notion of Christ as the sacrament of God immensely deepens sacramental theology. It under-

[4] T. A. Lacey, "Sacraments", *Encyclopedia of Religion and Ethics* (ed. J. Hastings), Edinburgh 1918, vol. X, col. 904.
[5] See J. de Ghellinck, *Pour l'histoire du mot* "Sacramentum", Louvain 1924, 75-140; "Mystére", *Dictionnaire Encyclopédique de la Bible*, Turnhout-Paris 1960, coll. 1230-1235.
[6] *Epistle* 187, 34, PL 38, 845.

lines the important fact that sacramentality is an essential part of
the divine economy of salvation. Once the sacraments are seen
as extensions of the *Ursakrament* which is Christ, as sources of
personal contact with the God-man, there is little danger of
regarding them merely as automatic or mechanical dispensers of
salvation *ex opere operato non ponentibus obicem*. But Christ
seen as sacrament of God has an even more significant aspect.
This approach underlines the altogether special place which the
humanity of Christ possesses in the salvation economy. For man
the humanity of Christ is more immediate and more "available"
than his divinity in that it is through Christ as man that we go to
the Father who is the source and term of the divine life and love
—*Per Christum*. Over-emphasis on the divinity of Christ to the
exclusion of the humanity places at a distance him who is our
brother, the first-born of the family of God. It also hides the
Trinitarian character of Christian spirituality—Christian life
becomes exclusively Christo-termed rather than theo-termed;
Christ becomes the end rather than the mediator. But the Gospels
and the apostolic tradition teach quite clearly that we go *Ad
Patrem per Filium in Spiritu Sancto*.

WHY A SACRAMENT?

Christ, the sacrament of God, has meaning only for one who
understands the nature of God's self-gift to man. In Adam by
a completely gratuitous act God called all men to personal
union with himself in grace in this life and the beatific vision in
eternity. This interpersonal encounter, this intimate union and
dialogue between God and man, is a strictly supernatural reality.
By Adam's sin this union was lost and man was helpless to regain
it by his unaided efforts. Certainly in the light of creation he
could attain to a knowledge of God as the absolute Being behind
changing things and could worship him as creator and lord of all.
Knowing the ultimate source of life to be a person, man could
envisage the possibility (but of course not the nature) of a more
personal union with God than that with which natural religion
supplied him—a communion between friend and friend beyond

the mere recognition and worship of the Creator by the creature. But this vague *velleitas* or nostalgia is the utmost reach of natural forces. It is only by revelation that the nature of this personal union can be made known, it is only by grace that it can be established—in both cases a completely benevolent approach on the part of God.

The divinizing principle or condition of the God-man union is sanctifying grace. This grace is to be conceived as something apart from the divine benevolence which causes it and the human response which welcomes it. It is a participation in the divine nature which assimilates the soul to God and in a manner deifies it ("divinae consortes naturae" 2 *Pet.* 1:4). It is the condition of that altogether familiar intimacy with God which is known as the divine indwelling, when the threefold God is present in the soul as the object of its love and contemplation.[7]

This indwelling of the Trinity is the primary and most important aspect of the state of grace. Man is led into the hidden life of God and shares in the union of love in which that life consists. Friendship is always between person and person, and so grace forges a special bond between the justified soul and each person of the Trinity. Charles Davis expresses the point well:

> Grace is in fact more than the production of a created effect (as such grace would relate us to God as one in nature). First and foremost it is God giving us himself. We are joined to God as he is in himself. . . . Such a relation (to the persons as distinct) does not offend against the unity of God any more than does the relation which the human nature of Christ has with God the Son alone.[8]

Leo XIII stated that this union by indwelling differs only by reason of our state from the union with God which the blessed enjoy in heaven,[9] and Pius XII has added that this vision of the blessed implies that they witness close at hand the processions of the divine persons and enjoy a beatitude very similar to that with which the most holy and undivided Trinity is blessed.[10]

[7] *S. theol.* I, q. 43, a. 3.
[8] *The Study of Theology*, London 1962, 140-1.
[9] Encyclical *Divinum Illud*, A.S.S. 39, 653.
[10] Encyclical *Mystici Corporis*, C.T.S. translation, 49.

Why does God open to us the life of the Trinity? Solely because he loves us. "What is man that thou are mindful of him?", asks the Psalmist with wonder (*Ps.* 8:5). This eternal divine love or *agape* is the Christian mystery at its most profound. This dynamic love is nothing else but God himself, the source of all life natural and supernatural. "God is love", says St John (1 *John* 4:16). In him alone is the quality of *bonum diffusivum sui* fully realized. It is in this love that the various sacraments of the Redemption and especially the Incarnation find their meaning.

If God wishes to initiate this supernatural union he must approach man who is helpless to come to him. This approach may take the form of a direct revelation and immediate outpouring of grace into man's heart. But the Fathers[11] and St Thomas[12] indicate that God in his normal providence wills to draw men to himself by the experience or intermediacy of sensible events. By sensible signs and incidents God intervenes in human life, and man makes his personal encounter with God in this intervention and in the grace there offered to him. And historically God has so intervened. Because these salvific interventions have assumed a visible and recognizable form it is proper to refer to them as sacraments—they are the signs and means of grace, of the personal religious union which God offers to men; sacrament in the Thomistic definition is "signum rei sacrae inquantum est sanctificans homines".[13]

THE SACRAMENT INITIATED

In the history of God's sacramental approach to man Christ stands at the pinnacle—every intervention before him is in prospect in that it is a figure and pledge of his coming, every intervention after him is in retrospect in that it unfolds his influence and meaning.

[11] "Si incorporeus esses, nuda tibi et incorporea dona (Deus) tribuisset, sed quia corpori coniuncta est anima, in sensibilibus spiritualia tibi largitur"— St John Chrysostom, *Homily on St Matthew*, 82, 4. PG 58, 743.

[12] "Pertinet autem ad divinam providentiam ut unicuique rei providet secundum modum suae conditionis; et ideo convenienter divina sapientia homini auxilia salutis confert sub quibusdam corporalibus et sensibilibus signis"—*S. theol.* III, q. 61, art. 1c.

[13] *S. theol.* III, q. 20, art. 2c.

Even to pagans God proferred the grace of a personal union. In his all-powerful providence he employed the things and truths of creation to instil in man a germinal revelation of his incomprehensible nature and to draw man to himself. "He left not himself without testimony", says St Paul, "doing good from heaven, giving rains and fertile seasons, filling our hearts with food and gladness" (*Acts* 14:16). Of course, it would be quite unwarranted to picture the religiosity of the pagan as of the purely natural order—fallen man could always hear in his inmost heart the distant restless call of the supernatural destiny which he once enjoyed and which is still in God's intention for him; in his myths he may have well preserved from the original revelation at the beginning of human history a residual presentiment of a Redeemer to come.[14] Then, too, under God's guiding hand material nature and the spiritual qualities in which man is the image of God would speak the language of salvation and become pointers to higher things.[15]

Of a truth the light of the Lord was ever shining in the darkness; it did not fully or extensively pierce the gloom of pagan insensibility, but it was effective to a degree: "Come", said St Clement af Alexandria to his pagan audience, "I will show you the Word ond the mysteries of the Word, and I will give you understanding of them by means of images familiar to you".[16]

These traces of divine revelation and intervention in pagan philosophy, myth and cult pale beside the striking concreteness of God's encounter with his chosen people. Israel was a great sacrament, a sign manifesting God's ever watchful providence and a visible offer of salvation. The salvific providence was evidenced by the choice, establishment and constant protection exercised by God in favour of this people. "I will be your God and you will be my people" is the recurring refrain of the Old Testament. He was near to them in their trials. The pillar of cloud by day and the pillar of fire by night which directed them through the wilderness (*Exod.* 13:23), the glory of God's majesty

[14] K. Rahner, *Theological Investigations*, I, London 1961, 302 f.
[15] Cf. *S. theol.* III, q. 61, art. 3, q. 103, art. 1.
[16] *Protrepticus* XII, 119, 1.

which filled the tabernacle (*Exod.* 40:32-6) were constant reminders of the Shekinah, the sheltering presence of God. The
intimate fellowship between God and the just soul which was
the result of this divine approach to man is described in the most
graphic terms by the sacred writers, terms which we still use
today: "As the hart pants after fountains of water, so my soul
pants after thee, O God" (*Ps.* 41:1); "The Lord is my shepherd
and I shall want nothing, he hath set me in a place of pasture"
(*Ps.* 22:1); surely, all this describes an initial return to that happy
state of divine friendship which Adam and Eve enjoyed when, as
the author of Genesis says, the Lord God walked in Paradise
taking the afternoon air.

This Israel with its believing people, its tabernacle, its sacraments was the first Church—a sign and source of divine grace
which drew its members into personal union with God, but
always in virtue of the Redeemer to come. This Church of God
was the archetype of the Church of Christ.[17] Indeed, the divine
activity exercised in the establishment of both Churches is
described in almost identical terms by Ezechiel (16:3-9) and by
St Paul (*Eph.* 5:25-7).

THE MYSTERY REALIZED

When the fullness of time was come God sent his Son (*Gal.*
4:4). This was the long-awaited Epiphany of the universal Saviour.
In him all the years of waiting and expectation would find their
meaning. St Paul calls this divine intervention the mystery of
Christ (*Rom.* 16:25, 1 *Cor.* 2:7, *Eph.* 1:9, 3:3-9, *Col.* 1:26, 2:2,
4:3). It is the plan of salvation conceived by God from all eternity
and finally revealed and realized in all its splendour in the person
of his Son. This theme permeates the gospel of St Paul; all its
phases and characteristics are especially detailed in the Captivity
Epistles (*Col.* 1; *Eph.* 1 & 3). Christ, the mystery of God, fulfils
all the promises and prophecies, manifests in the world to Jew
and Gentile the glory and the power of God, communicates to

[17] See J. Daniélou, *Sacramentum Futuri*, Paris 1950; *The Advent of Salvation*,
New York 1962.

men the love and knowledge of God, and as universal mediator
unites all men to God.

The Incarnation

In the Incarnation God becomes man—the dialogue between
God and man is realized in an undreamt of way. God in willing
that a bearer of the divine nature should become also a bearer
of the human nature extended to man the relationship of father-
hood in which he stands to his Son.

The mysterious make-up of this two-natured person is indicated
in the name *Christ*. In the Old Testament the Redeemer to come
is described frequently as the *Anointed* (e.g. *Ps.* 2:2, 44:8; *Dan.*
9:24; *Is.* 61:1). In *Acts* 10:38 God is said to have anointed Jesus
with the Holy Ghost and with power. This anointing is nothing
less than the fullness of the divinity of the Logos which permeates
the humanity of Christ, exalts it to the highest dignity and makes
it a fit vehicle of God's grace to men. "Christ is the name of the
person", says St John Damascene, "but the name also signifies
two natures. For he anointed himself; he anointed as God and
was anointed as man. He himself is both one and the other. The
ointment of the humanity is the divinity".[18]

One usually turns to St Paul for an understanding of the
nature of the divine intervention in the world in the person of
the Incarnate Word. But the mystery is evident in all the New
Testament authors and no one has a sublimer concept of it than
St John. For him Christ's coming is a sacrament of the eternal
love of the Father calling man to a mystical and most intimate
union. "God so loved the world as to give His only-begotten"
(*John* 3:16). The Prologue to the Fourth Gospel is a moving
description of the nature of this sacrament. The One who comes
is God the Son himself. He has been enlightening men's hearts
from the beginning by secret inspirations, now he comes personally to live among them, to reveal the love of God and to
unite men with the Father.

[18] *De fide orthodoxa* 3, 3. PG 94, 989. See M.-J. Scheeben, *The Mysteries of
Christianity*, London 1951, 331-4.

It was no haphazard chance that it was the second person of the Trinity who became man. God the Father in sending his Son into the world simply extended into the created order his eternal act of generation. The Incarnation continued the Father's act of self-giving by which he generates the Son.[19] In Christ men are called to become Sons of the Father—to enter the very life of the Trinity—to share in the divine life after the manner of the Son of God. Christ can call God "Father" by the unique privilege of his position—men can call God "Father" by becoming brothers and co-heirs with Christ.

Nothing could manifest God's love more visibly, more immeasurably, more effectively than this mission of the Son. More visibly: for what is more visible to man than a companion who is flesh and blood as he is? More immeasurably: for what more could God do than give his only-begotten Son? And more effectively: for once God became man the redemption was an inevitable reality as the old man Simeon knew: "Nunc dimittis servum tuum, Domine, quia viderunt oculi mei salutare tuum".

Beside this glorious Epiphany the earlier interventions of God in the thunder of Sinai and in the fiery words of the prophets fall silent: this advent, quiet as a gentle breeze, is the advent of God himself. St Paul highlights this pivotal point of history by a contrast with the gloomy state which obtained previously. Man was hopelessly doomed: the tyrant sin held sway over him; the flesh made him incapable of any resistance; death was inevitable. Then comes the new Adam abounding in grace to save all men. "By the Incarnation all men are embodied in God's Son and have become his members. He sees men in his Son, and his Son in all

---

[19] The Word is not alone the unique revealer of the Godhead but indeed the only revealer consonant with the relations in the Trinity. "Et sicut homo volens revelare se verbo cordis, quod profert ore, induit quodammodo ipsum verbum litteris vel voce, ita Deus, volens se manifestare hominibus, Verbum suum conceptum ab aeterno carne induit in tempore"—St Thomas, *In Joannem* 14, 2. "Comment un autre personne pouvait-elle révéler le Père mieux que cette Personne qui est la parfaite Image du Père, la parole qui épuise la connaissance que le Père a de lui-même? Et comment une autre Personne que le Fils pouvait-il révéler notre attitude filiale et nous apprendre à adorer le Père? Il convenait souverainement que le Verbe de Dieu en soit le Révélateur, et que le Fils du Père, son Amen, soit celui qui initie l'homme à sa vie filiale" —R. Latourelle, "Révélation, histoire et Incarnation", *Gregorianum* 44 (1963), 245. See also K. Rahner, "Réflexions théologiques sur l'Incarnation", *Sciences Ecclésiastiques* 12 (1960), 14.

men. Consequently they are worthy to be adopted as his children
and introduced into the divine family" (Scheeben).

Christ among men

If the Incarnation is the institution of Christ as the sacrament
of God, his life among men is the implementation of that sacrament. His very presence on earth is a sacrament in that it is at
once a manifestation of God's readiness to accept man and a
grant of the means to realize the union. In his visible humanity
Christ is willed by God as the only access to salvation: "For
there is only one mediator between God and man, the man
Christ Jesus" (1 *Tim.* 2:5). Only by contact with the humanity of
Christ can man cross the infinite void to the intimate union with
God which is grace and glory. "I am the way, the truth and the
life. No one comes to the Father but by me" (*John* 14:6).

The man Jesus has a plentitude of grace at his disposal because
of the hypostatic union—"In ipso complacuit omnem plenitudi-
nem inhabitare" (*Col.* 1:19). This plenitude is willed by God as
the source of grace for all men. All must receive it from him and
in the divine plan Christ dispenses it only through his humanity.

In the hypostatic union the human nature of Christ is deified
and made worthy of the task with which it is charged. So St
Thomas: "Humana natura non dicitur essentialiter dea sed
deificata—per coniunctionem ad divinam naturam in una
hypostasi".[20] Since the person who acts (*principium quod*) through
Christ's human nature possesses the omnipotence of the Godhead,
the human nature and its actions partake of the power of the
divinity. We can use the term "instrument", but one must be
careful to add that even when acting under the influence of the
divinity the mode of activity is typically human.[21] In Christ's
theandric activity there is nothing theatrical, no oracular enthusiasm; he simply touches the leper and that touch connaturally
cures in virtue of the divine power which is in him. All his grace-

[20] *S. theol.* III, q. 16, art. 3.
[21] "Humana natura in Christo non est tale instrumentum quod solum
agatur; sed quod etiam est principium actionis, inquantum habet dominium
sui actus"—St Thomas, *Quaestio unica de unione Verbi Incarnati* art. 5 ad 4.

giving contacts were simple human encounters; all his revelations were sober human words.

This role of the humanity casts new light on Christ's life among men. Every invitation "Come follow me", every suggestion "Go and do thou likewise", was an offer of grace. Every word or gesture could be a sacrament—"Thy sins are forgiven thee" (*Mark* 2:5), "Take up thy bed and walk, sin no more" (*John* 5:8-14), "And Jesus looked at Peter" (*Luke* 22:61). It is through his body and its faculties that man operates, manifests his will and spiritual powers, and makes contact with his fellows. So, too, in Christ. But in his case in virtue of the divine instrumentality which his humanity enjoyed the power which he exercised in his grace-giving actions was the power of the Godhead.[22] The emphasis on the humanity must never allow us to lose light of the fact that the encounter with Christ was always an encounter with a divine person; persons, not natures, meet. So when people responded to the invitation of the man Jesus they responded to God.

So far we have been dealing mainly with the human action of Christ as providing a mediation of God to men. This mediation in action was supplemented by a mediation in word in that the teaching of Christ was a reflection or communication to men of God's plan of salvation and of the hidden life within the Trinity to which man was called. The mission of the Son in the flesh is a continuation of his eternal procession from the Father—he goes forth from the Father in his own personal character and bears with him into the external world the relationship to the other persons which he has in the interior of the Godhead. This objective revelation of the community of love into which God had called men was specified and explained in the teaching of Christ, "Filius qui est in sinu Patris ipse enarravit" (*John* 1:18). He is not alone the Revealed of the father, he is also the Revealer. Again and again in the Gospels he speaks of the relation between the Father and himself, and between them both and the Holy Ghost. Truly St Paul could say: "God who commanded the light to shine out of darkness hath shined in our hearts to give the

---

[22] *S. theol.* I-II, q. 112, art. 1 ad 1.

light of the knowledge of the glory of God, in the face of Christ
Jesus" (2 *Cor.* 4:6).

Christ in his Pasch

In itself the Incarnation would seem to be the ultimate sacrament of God's love—"Semetipsum exinanivit formam servi
accipiens" (*Phil.* 2:7). The Lord of glory willingly foregoes all
the prerogatives of his divinity, and making common cause with
men imprisons himself in a human body. The Creator becomes
a creature. But love urges the incarnate God even further—Christ
takes on himself all the sins of humanity ("He was made sin for
us", 2 *Cor.* 5:21), and satisfies for them on the Cross. "Greater
love than this no man hath . . .". In the divine plan of salvation
these mysteries of Christ's Pasch have a special place. It was
specifically in his death and resurrection that the *transitus* from
death in sin to life in God was most concretely signified and
accomplished. The original kerygma emphasized this: "That
Christ died for our sins according to the Scriptures and that he
was buried and that he arose again the third day" (1 *Cor.* 15:3).

The apostles had been instructed by Christ concerning the
nature of his Hour, that his death would be the sacrament of the
union of all men in God: "I, if I be lifted up, will draw all things
to myself" (*John* 12:32). On the night before he suffered he
underlined the centrality of his passion when he left his disciples
a perpetual memorial of it. "This is my body which is given for
you"; "This is my blood of the New Testament which shall be
shed for many unto the remission of sins" (*Luke* 22:19, *Matt.*
26:28). The death of Christ now imminent will be a true expiatory
sacrifice which will definitively seal the alliance with God.

The resurrection is an essential part of this redeeming sacrament. On many occasions Christ had foretold this aspect of the
sign (*Matt.* 16:21, 17:9, 20:19; *Mark* 8:31, 9:8; *Luke* 9:22, 18:33)
—on the third day he will rise again. It would do less than justice
to the resurrection to regard it simply as a miracle, the supreme
proof of Christ's divinity. That it certainly is (see 1 *Cor.* 15:4),
but it is a great deal more. It belongs to the very essence of the

sacrifice of the passion in that it completes it as an efficacious sign. It is the victory over sin (*Christus victor mortis*), God's visible acceptance of the sacrifice of his Son, the full flowering of the hypostatic union; it consummates the alliance between God and men and establishes Christ as the *Kurios*, the glorified source of the new life now made available to the world.[23] "Humiliavit semetipsum factus obediens usque ad mortem, mortem autem crucis; propter quod et Deus exaltavit illum et donavit illi nomen quod est supra omne nomen" (*Phil.* 2:8-9). Christ returned to the Father is crowned with glory and honour and the full majesty of the divinity which he had laid aside (cf. *Phil.* 2:11, *Heb.* 2:9). He is God's radiant *Dynamis*; his sacred humanity is suffused with God's power making it a fit instrument for the dispensing of universal salvation.[24]

In the death and resurrection of the Saviour we must see not alone the signs and promises of the eventual justification of the human race but also its actual accomplishment. All men were vitally and personally implicated with Christ on Calvary: "Una enim oblatione consummavit in sempiternum sanctificatos" (*Heb.* 10:14).This theme is particularly evident in Paul's theology of justification. If the acts of Christ effect salvation it is because the whole race has died and risen in him in a redemption already accomplished. "One died for all", says the apostle, "accordingly all died" (2 *Cor.* 5:14). A clearer or more incisive statement of the position could not be desired. Men by a corporate solidarity constitute one moral person with Christ at the moment of his death. This common death to sin is not just a figure of speech; it is real for the Christian in that it changes his status and makes the most positive demands upon him: "Christ has died for all, therefore, those who live may not live any longer for themselves" (v. 15).

If the death of Christ is the sacrament of man's death to sin, his resurrection is the sacrament of his birth to the new life. The whole body of which Christ is the head has risen along with him. The triumph of Christ over sin and death is not a personal but a collective victory. Among the many Pauline texts which teach

[23] See Schillebeeckx, *Le Christ, Sacrement de la rencontre de Dieu*, 59 (E. tr. *Christ, the Sacrament of Encounter with God*).
[24] See O. Casel, op. cit. 144-5.

this doctrine the most striking is *Eph*. 2:5-6: "Even when we were dead in sin, he has made us alive together with Christ, and has raised us up with Christ and has seated us in heaven together with and in Christ".[25]

Christ, man's response to God

In this treatment of Christ as the sacrament of God we have detailed one side of the encounter between God and man, namely, man's salvation. But we must not forget the other side, namely, man's response. Dialogue is always reciprocal. In the Incarnation of his Son God makes his most generous approach to men, and in turn he meets with the most generous response. In Christ God encountered his infinite glorification. "Only the Son, identical in nature with the Father, is able to honour and glorify God in his entire greatness. He alone as the Father's essential Word can express the entire majesty of the Father".[26] Christ as man fully responded to God's will for union. In him alone was found that fidelity which God had sought in vain in the old alliance: "I have come to do thy will, O Lord" (*Heb*. 10:7). In one and the same person were manifested the generosity of the divine invitation and the human acceptance, and in this intimate union of natures and wills was symbolized and established that rapport between God and man which all men find in grace. The response of Christ was the response of all mankind. He was the High-Priest; his prayer of adoration, thanksgiving and reparation was the prayer of God's newly-sanctified people.

THE SACRAMENT COMPLETED

"Et homo factus est—et ascendit in coelum". These words of the Creed mark the terms of the earthly life of Christ, of the duration of God's visit to his people in his visible human nature.

[25] *S. theol.* III, q. 56, art. 2 ad 4. See F. Holtz, "La valeur sotériologique de la Résurrection du Christ selon saint Thomas", *Eph. Theol. Lovan*. 26 (1953), 632.
[26] Scheeben, op. cit., 358.

He left with a promise—"I go to prepare a place for you—and
I will come again and will take you to myself" (*John* 14:3). Christ
in his resurrection and ascension becomes the majestic *Kurios*
—his humanity now suffused with the glory of the Godhead
receives a universal life-giving force. He sends forth the promised
Paraclete to sanctify all men, giving them the grace of divine
adoption: "Misit Deus Spiritum Filii sui in cordibus nostris
clamantem: Abba Pater" (*Gal.* 4:6; *Rom.* 8:16). Of course, the
Spirit was always present in Christ but in the divine plan his
activity was limited in the days of Christ's mortal flesh; his full
effects were not produced until after the resurrection: "Nondum
enim erat Spiritus datus, quia Jesus nondum erat glorificatus"
(*John* 7:39). So in this final stage of the Kingdom of God on earth
the Spirit is especially active in drawing men to God through
Christ. It is the function of the Spirit, the bond of love between
Father and Son, to unite men to Christ and to bring them to the
Father through Christ. This is the second phase of the journey
of the divine love—previously out from the Father, through the
Son and in the Holy Ghost, and now back by the action of the
Holy Spirit through the Son to the Father.

In the return journey to the Father Christ is again the sacrament
of God—"No one comes to the Father but by me" (*John* 14:6)
—*Per Christum ad Patrem*. Perhaps this may sound strange to
those who see the theological significance of Christ primarily in
his divinity, the term of adoration and prayer. But Christ pointed
always beyond himself to the Father, and it was to him that he
directed all his prayer. Why? Because in all his salvific activity
Christ is a mediator, the way to the Father. This is the constant
teaching of the apostolic Church: "There is one God, and one
mediator of God and man, the man Christ Jesus" (1 *Tim.* 2:5);
"We have an advocate with the Father, Jesus Christ the Just"
(1 *John* 2:2). Hence the primitive Christian formula "In the name
of Jesus"—"Giving thanks always for all things, in the name of
Our Lord Jesus Christ, to God and the Father" (*Eph.* 5:20); "All
things do ye in the name of the Lord Jesus Christ, giving thanks
to God and the Father by him" (*Col.* 3:17); "That in all things
God may be honoured through Jesus Christ" (1 *Peter* 4:11); "I
give thanks to my God through Jesus Christ" (*Rom.* 1:8).

In the year 393 the Synod of Hippo, at which St Augustine was present, decreed in its 21st canon: "Semper ad Patrem dirigatur oratio".[27] This did not deny that Christ was God, identical in nature with the Father as a source of grace, but it indicated that the prayer of the Church should be modelled on that of its Head and should be directed through him to the Father. The Roman liturgy well preserves this doctrine of Christ, the mediator and high priest, in that it concludes all its prayers with the clause *Per Christum Dominum nostrum*.

It is not our purpose here to detail the decline of this heritage in theology and popular devotion. Father Jungmann[28] finds the chief cause in the Arian heresy. By denying the Son's divinity and essential equality with the Father this heresy called forth a strong and extreme reaction among Catholics. In the Eastern liturgies the primitive clausula "Through Christ Our Lord" was no longer acceptable. St Basil and St Athanasius changed the ancient doxology "Glory be to the Father through the Son and in the Holy Ghost" to "Glory be to the Father with the Son and with the Holy Ghost" or to "Glory be to the Father and to the Son and to the Holy Ghost". Throughout the Eastern Christian world the sense of the centrality of Christ's humanity in our redemption was overlaid—he became the awful Lord, remote from his people, hidden behind the iconostasis. In his presence man prostrates obsessed by the thought of his sin and unworthiness. There is little here of the gentle Christ who took the children on his knee, and who in his agony prayed for his enemies and pardoned the Good Thief. To fill the void left by the withdrawal of Our Lord's humanity, veneration of the saints attained an unprecedented importance. In present-day theology, however, there has developed a fuller appreciation of Our Lord's humanity and a return to the balanced faith of the early Church which saw all salvation as an approach to God in and with Christ.

Here a problem strikes us: how is the encounter with the man Christ possible now that he has left the earth? Certainly the glorified humanity of Christ as an instrument of the divinity

---

[27] "Ut nemo in precibus vel Patrem pro Filio, vel Filium pro Patre nominet. Et cum altari assistitur, semper ad Patrem dirigatur oratio" (Mansi III, 922).

[28] *Die Stellung Christi im liturgischen Gebet*, Münster 1925, 103-51. See also K. Adam, *Christ Our Brother*, London 1931, 51-9.

could immediately influence souls without the necessity of any
visible intermediary. But, as we have said, man's earthly limited
nature demands a visible mediation of God—in other words, a
sacrament. Here we stand on the threshold of the mystery of the
Church. Sacramentality, justification by visible means, is ever
preserved as the order of God's economy of salvation. The
visible presence of the incarnate Word returned to his Father is
continued by the visible presence of his mystical body, the Church.
"The Word is made flesh", says St Augustine in a striking sentence, "in order to become the head of the Church".[29] The Church
is a sacrament, a visible sign and principle of grace, because it is
a continuation of the sacrament of Christ.

Christ may have physically left this earth, his death and
resurrection may be historically past—but both the glorified Lord
and his saving actions are still present in the Church in a most
real way. The glorified humanity of Christ still bearing the marks
of his passion is a lasting sacrament "semper vivens ad interpellandum pro nobis" (*Heb.* 7:25); it is the unique source of
grace, and that grace is always conferred in virtue of the acts
of his passion. As in the accomplishment of the universal redemption so too in the justification of the individual soul Christ's
humanity acts as agent of the divinity—as an efficient though
instrumental cause of grace. Informed by the *virtus divina* it is
deified—its mode of action is essentially divine knowing no limit
of time or space. Making provision for the time when he would
no longer be among men in his bodily form, Christ selected
certain symbols to indicate and continue the grace-giving action
of his humanity. So, even if Christ, the primary sacrament, is no
longer among men, the *virtus divina* of his sacred humanity
(*instrumentum coniunctum*) is still conferring grace through the
visible sacraments (*instrumenta separata*)[30] which he instituted to
perpetuate his saving presence. "Quod conspicuum erat in
Christo transivit in Ecclesiae sacramenta", says St Leo.[31] And

[29] *On Psalm* 148, 8. PL 37, 1942.
[30] *S. theol.* III, q. 62, art. 5. On the *virtus divina* which informs the
humanity of Christ and his sacraments see Holtz, op. cit., 624-7, and the most
important study by P. Wegenaer, *Heilsgegenwart, die Heilswerk Christi und
die Virtus Divina in den Sakramenten unter besonderer Berücksichtigung von
Eucharistie und Taufe*, Münster 1958.
[31] *Sermo* 74.2. PL 54, 398.

even more vividly St Ambrose—"Facie ad faciem te mihi, Christe, demonstrasti, in tuis te invenio sacramentis".[32] It was not by chance that St Thomas placed his tract on the sacraments immediately after his treatment of Christ's life and passion. He refers to the sacraments as *sacramenta humanitatis*,[33] because they are the acts of Christ in his human nature, his personal acts— just as personal as his act of touching the eyes of the man born blind. Pius XII says in *Mystici Corporis*: "It is Christ who baptizes ... it is Christ who absolves ... it is Christ who offers". In a very real way Christ is present in the sacraments—this presence is most real and actual in the Eucharist in that he is present there body, blood, soul and divinity by transubstantiation, but he is present in the other sacraments also in that they continue his human activity.

This emphasis on the sacraments as acts of the glorified Christ may seem to minimize the position of the passion as the source of all grace. But, of course, there is no question of separating the glorified Christ from Christ in the days of his flesh. The humanity of Christ has become the glorified principle of grace through the passion;[34] every grant of grace made by the glorified Lord is made through and in virtue of the mysteries of his Pasch. In the redeeming actions of Christ there is some element which is permanent and independent of all limits of space and time, something which gives these actions an universally actual salvific efficacy.

Christ in the mysteries of his passion exercises an efficient salvific causality which transcends time and space. It is these very mysteries, or rather the dying and rising Christ, which actually sanctify souls in the sacrament. Since there is question not of physical contact but of a *contactus virtutis divinae* the distance between the source and the term is of no significance. The redemption is reactualized not, of course, in its physical historical circumstances, not in the too real substantial sense alleged in the *Mysterienlehre* of Odo Casel, but in the sense that the humanity of Christ and his saving acts are present actively and dynamically

---

[32] *Apologia Prophetae David* 12, 58. PL 14, 875.
[33] *S. theol*. III, q. 80, art. 5. See *Mediator Dei*, A.A.S. 39 (1947), 533.
[34] See Wegenaer, op. cit., 15. K. O'Shea, "Sacramental Realism: The acrifice of the Mass", *Irish Theol. Quart*. 30 (1963), 128.

in the sacrament. The *virtus divina* acts in and through them to effect the justification of the individual soul.[35] In the world of the supernatural and of the sacrament this is as real a presence as can or need be.

St Paul shows a vivid appreciation of this presence of the Saviour in the sacrament in his description of Christian baptism. In baptism salvation-history becomes actual for the individual. In baptism we die with Christ (*Rom.* 6:8), we are crucified with him (*Rom.* 6:6, *Gal.* 2:9), we are buried with him (*Rom.* 6:4, *Col.* 2:12). It would be quite unwarranted to see these συν-verbs merely or chiefly as symbols and figures drawn from the rite of baptism by immersion. This would be to read into Paul the symbols and figures of a later and decadent theology. Paul's statements are strictly doctrinal—perhaps there is a word-play on the immersion symbol in *consepulti* (*Rom.* 6:4; *Col.* 2:12), but if so it is purely by the way. For the apostle baptism is essentially man's personal union with the Saviour, his personal undertaking of the *transitus* in union with the dying and rising Christ. This is the significance of the phrases "Baptism into Christ", "Baptism into the death of Christ"—"As many of you as have been baptized in Christ Jesus have been clothed with Christ" (*Gal.* 3:27). Baptism, through association with the Saviour, leads to the mystical union of God and man in Christ—"Vita vestra est abscondita cum Christo in Deo" (*Col.* 3:3). This *transitus* in union with the Saviour is so real to St Paul that he cannot comprehend any backsliding on the part of the Christian: "We who are dead to sin, how shall we still live in it" (*Rom.* 6:2). Paul has recourse here not to the "Thou shalt not" of the preacher, but to the simple "Thou art" of the theologian who is deeply conscious of the power and finality of the encounter with God in Christ.

---

[35] "Die effiziente Ursachlichkeit der Menschheit Christi ist in die Sakramente übergegangen. Auf Grund der Einsetzung durch Christus bedient sich die *virtus divina* der Sakramente als *instrumenta separata* zur Verwicklichung des Heils. Die göttliche Kraft, die dem geschichtlichen Christusmysterium, d.h. Christus und seiner *passio*, die nicht an Raum und Zeit gebundene Wirksamkeit verleiht, ist auch jetzt im Sakrament die Brücke zwischen der vergangenen Heilstat und den Menschen. Denn auch von der im Sakrament gegenwärtigen *virtus divina* muss man sagen, dass sie *praesentialiter* alle Orte und Zeiten erreicht"—Wegenaer, op. cit., 41.

CONCLUSION

Christianity is not a doctrine, it is a person; it is not a theology, it is a history. "I preach Christ", says St Paul, "And Christ crucified" (1 *Cor.* 1:23). It centres on a unique act of divine self-revelation—the Incarnation, life, death and resurrection of the second person of the Trinity. Man strive as he might could never attain the grace of union with the Godhead—so God in an act of supreme generosity willed to bring man to himself. This he could have done directly and immediately but he chose a way more consonant with the nature of his creature, the way of visible intervention, the way of the sacrament. The sacrament provides the personal encounter with God—in it God proffers to men the invitation and means of coming to him, and man goes to God in a welcoming response. The sacrament is the very condition of the dialogue between the God of heaven and the man of earth.

God's love for men urged him to choose a sacrament that which no greater can be imagined—the Son of God himself becomes man. Christ, the sacrament of God, is infinitely significant and infinitely efficacious. Infinitely significant in that his coming and his whole life signify most strikingly God's salvific providence and his will to save men. Infinitely efficacious in that the encounter with his sacred humanity is the infallible encounter with God: "If any man love me . . . my Father will love him, and we will come to him and make our abode with him" (*John* 14:23).

The humanity of Christ and the mysteries of his redemption are the basic sacrament of man's salvation. Christ returned to God in glory continues his sacramental intervention in the Church; the sacrament of the Church is the ever-widening arc of the sacrament of Christ. In it and in the sacramental rites instituted by him he continues to be truly and actively present among men. Sacramentality is at the very heart of Christianity —far from seeming an obstacle it should appear as the very means and mode of the Saviour's direct encounter with those he came to save. The individual acts of sacramental sanctification are just as truly theandric acts of Christ as are his passion and death. Indeed, they all form one series with the passion and death. As distinct acts they succeed one another in time, but in themselves and by the will of their author they are ordered to the one term —the redemption of the human race.

This basic appreciation of the sacrament as transparent with Christ and his passion can easily be lost sight of in an exclusive preoccupation with the mechanics of sacramental causality, *ex opere operato* efficacy, conditions for validity and lawfulness. All these are essential to a Christian theology but they must serve to specify and enhance the Christic character of the sacrament as an act of Christ and as an encounter with God.

The Sacramental System

WE should do well to begin the meditation of our topic by
reminding ourselves of the picture drawn by Luther in one
of his most polemical writings, the *De Captivate Babylonica*, to
describe what the Church and its sacraments had become in his
eyes at the time. He said that the image projected by the Church
was that of an enormous pumping machine supposed to enable
us to draw upon the merits of Christ and the saints, and to this
end terminating in seven large taps. By every one of these taps,
he says, stands a priest who is ready to turn it and make it give
a few drops every time somebody comes and pays the right fee.

Of course, this is a very gross caricature, but is there some
trace in it of what we do to the sacraments, through our too facile
description of them as seven parallel channels distributing grace
to mankind by the ministration of the priests? Is this more or
less how they appear in the routine of our daily practice? I think
the best which can be said is that to the average Christian the
Church with its seven sacraments appears as a kind of big spiritual
supermarket or cafeteria. As he sees it, there are there seven
different counters to which he may go to fulfil his various needs.
Then he has only to choose what is needed, with the help of the
competent assistant, and after that to "cash and carry"! Whether
he will consume the goods provided for him on the spot or at

home, nobody has a right to care. It follows that he has not even
a vague idea that the different sacraments are simply connected
parts in an organic whole, and still less that the Church is something more than just the organisation which caters for the sus-
tenance of his own individual life, that it is the living organism
in which the Christian life is nurtured in community.

Now the best way to replace that false view of the Church and
of the sacraments by the right one is to start from the close connection not only between these entities themselves but between
them and the divine word.

The word of God, especially when we see it coming to its
fullness in the mystery of Christ, is indeed the richest of realities;
it has all the variety of life, but nothing can be more deeply one,
for it is one with the unity of a unique personality—that of Christ,
and with the singleness of one act once for all accomplished—
the saving event of his Cross. And the sacraments are not so
much, as is sometimes said, seven facets of a single crystal
through which the same living light and warmth of the mystery
is refracted, but they are rather the constituent elements of a
circulatory system through which the same life-giving blood is
constantly diffusing from and concentrating back on a central
focus, which is the heart of the mystical body. This focus, this
pulsing heart is the Mass. For the Mass is not only the source
of the whole sacramental order, as St Thomas says, because it
contains the passion of Christ, source of all graces, it is also
that which draws back to itself the whole life diffused through the
members, so that in them all and from them all it tends to unity
no less than it proceeds from unity.

The sacramental order, as a means to an end, is to disappear
on the last day. But there is something in the Mass that is to last
for ever—what St Thomas calls the *res tantum*, that is to say that
union of the mystical body which, when it has come to its perfection, will never more need either the *sacramentum*, the visible
elements and the ritual that handles them, or the *sacramentum
et res*, the sacramental presence of Christ under them. We can
say even more: not only the consummated union of the mystical
body, now achieved in its Head "known" by us as we have been

known by him from the first, will survive the sacramental order itself, but also that which is in the Mass of "eucharist" properly so-called will similarly survive. For the Eucharist is both the eucharistic prayer of the preface and canon and the eucharistic consecration imbedded in it. And the eucharistic prayer is the response which the Word of God announced to us is to evoke, while the eucharistic consecration is the self-dedication of the full Christ, Head and body, to the Father perfectly "known" in the Son of God who has become also the Son of Man. Let us try to go deeper into these two inseparable truths.

What was the Word's coming to us to achieve? It was to create the people of God in the mystical body of the Son of God made man, to reconcile man with the Father in his own body offered on the Cross. As St Augustine says in the last pages of his *City of God*:

> Adam himself lies now scattered on the whole surface of the earth. Formerly concentrated in one place he has fallen; having been broken to pieces, as it were, he has filled the universe with his debris. However, God's mercy has gathered together from everywhere his fragments and by fusing them in the fire of his charity, has reconstituted their broken unity.

This beautiful image is familiar to all the Fathers. It could be found already in Origen. And it has its foundation in thoughts clearly expressed by St John and still more explicitly by St Paul. It is what lies behind that sentence of the High Priest quoted and commented upon by St John: "It is expedient for you that one man should die for the people", which he explains by saying: "He did not say this of his own accord, but being high priest that year he prophesied that Jesus should die for the nation, and not for the nation only, but to gather into one the children of God who are scattered abroad" (11:51-2). But the thought is more strikingly expressed in what St Paul says in the first Epistle to the Corinthians, chapter 15, when he calls Jesus not only a second Adam, but the last Adam, which means the last man. That is to say, just as from the father Adam we have proceeded by a kind of fragmentation, so, in the heavenly man, we are to be made one again.

And this is exactly what the Eucharist, as he explains in the same epistle, is to achieve. As he says in the tenth chapter: "The bread which we break, is it not a participation in the body of Christ? Because there is one loaf, we who are many are one body, for we all partake of the same loaf". And, in the Epistle to the Ephesians, he will go further into the same thought by presenting the end, the goal of the whole life of the Church and of all the Christians in it, as "building up the body of Christ until we all attain to the unity of the faith and of the knowledge of the Son of God, to mature manhood, to the measure of the stature of the fullness of Christ" (4:12-13).

However, and this is our second point, this unity of the full body of Christ to be achieved through the eucharistic life of the Church is not a static but a dynamic unity, for it is the unity of God's own love, "shed abroad into our hearts by the Spirit" (*Rom.* 5:5). It is the unity of that love which comes down from the Father to the Son and ascends back to the Father with the Son himself in the Holy Spirit. Through that love, which is the inner life of the Trinity, as Dionysius of Rome said in his epistle to Dionysius of Alexandria: "the Trinity proceeds from the Father into the Son, to be recapitulated with the Son into the Father through the Holy Spirit". Now, because the Son has been made man, in his body crucified, risen again and become "spiritual", the same flowing down of the divine love brings us all together into this body to be there with the Son taken back unto the Father in the divine rapture of the Spirit.

Now this is what the eucharistic prayer means and the eucharistic consecration makes possible. By joining in the eucharistic prayer we acknowledge the love of God for us, manifested first in creation but "commended to us" above all, as St Paul says, in the Cross of Christ. And through the eucharistic consecration we are assumed into the self-dedication of Christ to his Father, so that there may be realized, as he indicated in his priestly prayer in the concluding chapters of St John, the end of his own sacrifice. "I sanctify myself, that is to say I consecrate myself through the Cross—so that they also be sanctified (or consecrated) in truth" (17:19).

In fine, this which is now in the process of accomplishment

through the sacramental offering of the Mass is that which is to remain permanently "in truth" when all the sacraments will have disappeared into eternity as the light of the stars into the light of day. It is the immortal state which will then be that of the whole mystical body, as it is now already the eternal state of Christ's humanity in the immediate presence and glory of the Father "*Semper vivens ad interpellandum pro nobis*".

Here lies the explanation of that constant saying of the Fathers of the Church, that it is the Eucharist which brings back the hundredth lost sheep of humanity to the choir of the ninety-nine sheep of the angelic hosts, who have never ceased from contemplating the face of God and rendering to him their homage of praise and adoring love. Reciprocally, it explains why Holy Scripture, from *Isaias* (ch. 6) to *Apocalypse* (chs. 4 and 5) describes heavenly life as a perpetual eucharist—the Seraphim singing incessantly "Holy, Holy, Holy the Lord Sabaoth; the earth is full of his glory"; the elders (who are the guardian angels and first priests of creation) throwing their crowns before the throne, having harps in their hands and golden bowls full of the incense of the prayers of the saints, adding to the eternal hymn of praise the new song of the Lamb:

> Worthy art thou to take the scroll and to open its seals, for thou wast slain and by thy blood didst ransom man for God, for every tribe and tongue and people and nation, and hast made them a kingdom and priest to our God and thou shalt reign on earth (*Apoc.* 5:9-10).

However, it is not the natural man, the scattered members of the fallen Adam, who is able to take part in that eucharistic life of praise and consecration in and to the divine love. For any man to be able to do so there is need of a new birth which will bring him to a new kind of being, a new way of life no longer earthly but heavenly. This can be achieved only through death to that old self inherited from Adam and resurrection into the new man that is Christ. Hence baptism and confirmation; they are to be seen as an initiation to the eucharistic celebration, understood with that fullness of meaning and action which we have just tried to express. That is to say they enable us to take on a new Christian

being, which is what St Paul calls "being in Christ", with the
effect of participating in the royal and priestly unction of Christ,
the unction of the Holy Spirit.

Baptism and confirmation, then, are nothing else than the
immediate preparation to take part in the Eucharist, as was so
clearly taught by the ancient practice of giving them together in
the Paschal celebration as a preliminary to the Paschal Mass itself.
On the other hand, baptism and confirmation are to be seen not
so much as two separate sacraments as the two complementary
poles of a single transformation of our being into the new being
in Christo Jesu. In baptism is emphasized the aspect of death
leading to resurrection with Christ. As St Paul says:

> Do you not know that all of us who have been baptized into
> Christ Jesus were baptized into his death? We were buried
> therefore with him by baptism into death, so that as Christ
> was raised from the dead by the glory of the Father, we too
> might walk in newness of life. For if we have been united
> with him in a death like his, we shall certainly be united with
> him in a resurrection like his. We know that our old self was
> crucified with him, so that the sinful body might be destroyed,
> and we might no longer be enslaved to sin. For he who has
> died is free from sin. But, if we have died with Christ, we
> believe that we shall also live with him. For we know that
> Christ being raised from the dead will never die again, death
> no longer has dominion over him. The death he died, he
> died for sin, once for all, but the life he lives, he lives for
> God. So you also must consider yourselves dead to sin and
> alive to God in Christ Jesus" (*Rom.* 6:3, 11).

All that St Paul will sum up again in his Epistle to the
Colossians, read in part in the Paschal Vigil:

> In him, the whole fullness of deity dwells bodily and you
> have come to fullness of life in him, who is the head of all
> rule and authority. In him also you were circumcized with a
> circumcision made without hands, by putting off the body
> of flesh in the circumcision of Christ, and you were buried
> with him in baptism, in which you were also raised with

him through faith in the working of God, who raised him
from the dead. . . . If then you have been raised with Christ,
seek the things that are above where Christ is, seated at the
right hand of God. Set your minds on things that are above,
not on things that are on earth. For you have died and your
life is hid with Christ in God. When Christ who is our life
appears, then you also will appear in glory" (*Col.* 2:9-12,
3:1-4).

But this new man which emerges from death to newness of
life in baptism, because he is now and forever in Christ will live
by the very unction which constitutes the *Christ*, that is to say
the anointed one. This is the proper meaning and content of
confirmation. It is not any gift of the Spirit, nor is it just the gift
of some spiritual strength needed to defend our faith from the
attacks of the enemy (that was already the gift pertaining to the pre-
baptismal unction). It is a consecration of our whole being, body
and soul, to be now and forever a temple, the temple of the
Spirit. It means that the presence of the Spirit in us is no longer
to be something accidental or transient but that he is to dwell in
us permanently. This "Temple of the Spirit" is not just a pictur-
esque figure for any kind of receptacle; it signifies, as the Fathers
have it, a vessel which will take to itself forever the fragrance of
the anointment. That is to say we are to be now for the Spirit
an animated temple of which he himself will be the soul. He is
to dwell in us therefore properly as the gift of the Father in the
Son, just as he is in the life of the Trinity the gift, the *Donum*
of the Father to the Son, through which at the same time the Son
surrenders himself to the Father.

Thus it is that we are to be anointed just like Christ the Anointed
One, so that we are in actual reality associated with this royal
priesthood.

This association is to be manifested in the part we are now to
play in the eucharistic celebration. The immediate consequence
of baptism and confirmation in the ancient Church was not only
introduction into the Church in general, but introduction precisely
into that celebration. As we have said already, in the Paschal
Night, the newly-baptized and confirmed, having been received
into the Christian fellowship by the bishop's kiss of peace, were

immediately led by him to the gathering of the whole people of God, now ready to offer the Paschal Eucharist. In that Eucharist, the neophytes were no longer just to attend, and that in the first part only. They were now to take part—not only to receive some spiritual gifts they could not receive before, but to be actively engaged in the celebration itself as component and integral parts of the wholly active body in a way really "priestly".

Now how is that to be understood? For the Fathers it signified more than interior adhesion to what the bishop or priest was to do, more than mere participation in responses or singing. It meant exactly and precisely three things which we find, time and again, mentioned, explained, insisted upon in all the catechetical literature of antiquity. It meant, as they said, to pray, to offer, to communicate. In that threefold action the role of the kingly priesthood in the Eucharist eminently consisted.

Now by *prayer* the Fathers were always careful to explain that what was intended was a kind of prayer which can be prayed only by a baptized and anointed Christian. The catechumens, they stated, could not yet pray in that way. For it is the prayer of a true member of Christ, who has in himself the Spirit of adoption, so that in truth he may dare to address God as "Father". But it must be understood that this prayer was not just a mere repetition or union in the prayer of the Church. It was an act both entirely personal and fully public, which was to take place not as an individual association in a pre-existing liturgy, but as an integral element of that very liturgy. In the liturgy and understood as most essential parts of it, there were moments of silent prayer, especially after the hearing of God's word. Everyone then was urged by the priest and deacon to pray, that is to make his own individual and irreplaceable response to the word of God. And let us insist: this was not considered a break in the liturgy, or a mere appendage to it; it was seen as an integral part of it, as the primary and fundamental part to be played in it by the baptized and confirmed Christian. So that their most personal prayer in their own words or in pure silence was not just a private prayer. It was con- stituted an essential element of the public prayer itself. You had not then alongside the liturgy seen as an official and impersonal prayer, the personal prayer of the faithful, having maybe a close relation to it in its substance, but foreign to it. Within the liturgy itself the personal prayer was not only admitted but there was no idea that a liturgy of the Church could exist without that.

After prayer came *oblation*, which means the material offering of bread and wine for the eucharist. But in it was implied and in some way expressed an offering to Christ of our life—in its very principles, in the food that is to sustain it—so that he might transform it into his own crucified and renewed life. This, let us notice, was not the adjunction of a sacrifice of our own to the unique sacrifice of Christ. It was rather, on the analogy of prayer as accepting personally the word of God in obedient faith, our consent that Christ should take us into his own sacrifice.

When that has been done, the third and last act of participation can be realized—*communion*, that is to say the consummation of our union with Christ in his sacrifice, so that we may be renewed in our membership of his mystical body by being fed again from his risen body.

Now all through it must be clear that this exercise of the royal priesthood of all the members in the Eucharist is dependent on the two priestly actions which nobody except Christ can do for the Church, namely, the ceaselessly renewed announcement of the word of the gospel, the no less perpetual re-presentation in the sacrament of this unique sacrifice. It is from the first that the Christian prayer takes its inspiration, while it is the second alone that can consecrate our offering so that we may be able finally to communicate. Hence comes the necessity for the sacrament of order, since one must preserve permanently present in the gathering of the Church at the Eucharist Christ as the word announced and as priest and victim of the sacrifice there offered. The bishop and the priest are ordained principally to be able to take the role of the head in the gathering of the body to bring to it both the word announced and the word of power and of the Spirit which consecrates the sacrifice. But that cannot be accomplished otherwise than by Christ catching hold of them; so to speak, to use them as his instruments, so that the words they will say, the deeds they will do, will not only be the same words and deeds which were said and done by Christ, but in very truth here and now will be said and done by Christ himself.

Ordination itself takes place in the Mass, and ordination to the priesthood just before the announcement of the Gospel, so that the Church will be provided with ministers of the word and ministers to consecrate the sacrifice of the whole body made one with its Head.

Penance in its turn has a no less intimate connection with the Mass. Just as the sacraments of initiation are an introduction to Christianity in so far as they adapt us for participation in the eucharistic celebration, penance is properly the restoration of the same capacity in those who have lost it by any grievous sin. Nothing could have manifested it more clearly than the ancient rite for the public reconciliation of penitents, as it is still fully described in the Roman Pontifical. On Maundy Thursday, just before the Mass in commemoration of the Lord's Supper, the bishop went to the door of the Church to meet there the penitents excommunicated until then. To reconcile them both with God and his Church he took them by the hand and brought them back to their former place in the ranks of the faithful now gathered for the Eucharist so that they might participate again in its celebration.

However, it is no less important to see the relation of the Eucharist to the whole of Christian life, outside the Church as well as inside, than to see its relation to the other sacraments— or rather their relation to the Eucharist. The kingly priesthood of the whole body of the Church, made possible by the transmission of the apostolic ministry through ordination and exercised first of all in the eucharistic celebration, is to impose its pattern on the whole of Christian life, on the life of the layman as well as on that of the priest, although in a different fashion. And this pattern is to be not only sacramental, but more precisely eucharistic. It is to be sacramental because it means that having taken part in the sacramental life we shall be capable of transforming everything into a means by which God's grace will become real in us and be made active in the world at large through us. It will be eucharistic because it will take the form of an acknowledgment on the part of our faith that everything comes to us from God and is God's word of love to us, and consequently it will take the form also of a consecration by our own activity informed by

charity of the whole world as an instrument of praise, an offering
of love.

But that consecration of our whole life by the sacramental
energy will be directly fostered by the last two sacraments, holy
matrimony and extreme unction. They may be said to be a
consecration of both natural human fecundity and infirmity.
This they do by introducing in some way both human creative
love and human "illness unto death" into the circle of grace and
love which is that of the Eucharist. This is highlighted in a remarkable manner by the fact that extreme unction is to be conferred
with an oil consecrated in the Mass just before the *Per quem haec
omnia* at the end of the Canon, a prayer which was formerly meant
to convey—and as it were diffuse from the Eucharist itself—
the blessing of God on all the fruits of the earth. Similarly, the
nuptial blessing (which is a blessing of the fruitfulness of human
love in the woman) is to take place also during Mass, and just
before communion.

Here we see how the sacramental and eucharistic life is to
assume both our natural life and death into the fulfilment of
Christ in his body the Church. The consecration of human love
in matrimony and of the whole family life through it, means a
consecration of the whole of human creation and endeavour into
the fullness of Christ. But on the other hand, the unction of the
sick is a consecration of human agony into a participation in the
passion of Christ himself. However that does not mean just a
consecration of natural life on the one hand and of natural death
on the other. The consecration of human life in matrimony falls
under the shadow of the Cross, since as St Paul says in the
Epistle to the Ephesians which is read in the Mass *Pro Sponso et
Sponsa*, man is to love his wife "as Christ loved the Church and
gave himself up for her", while the consecration of human
suffering in the sacrament of the sick is intended as a power, so
that we may be cured from all the effects of sin on our nature and
be prepared for the final triumph in us of life over death itself.
Therefore, through both these sacraments, we have the promise
of the ultimate identification which is the end of all the sacramental order, the identification of our fallen being through the
mystery of the Cross with the glorious being of Christ risen again
and living forever "to the glory of the Father".

Acts of Christ: Signs of Faith[1]

CORNELIUS ERNST

INTRODUCTION

IN a recent article on the catechesis of the sacraments, the writer, a Canadian Dominican, lays down two principles for the presentation of the sacramental mystery; firstly, that "every sacrament is a saving event"; secondly, "that this event is brought about by means of a sign-of-faith".[2] I do not wish now to examine the correctness of such a view, with which I am in general agreement, but merely to ask just what catechumens, and indeed just what catechists, the writer has in mind. When I think of the great body of Catholics both clerical and lay, in England (I cannot of course speak for Ireland), I am afraid my mind simply reels at the thought of persuading them to think about the sacraments in the way described; on the other hand, when I think of a growing

---

[1] I should like to acknowledge here a general debt to the writings of E. H. Schillebeeckx, O.P., far greater than can be indicated by explicit citations. *De sacramentele Heilseconomie*, Antwerp-Bilthoven 1952; *Christus, Sacrament van de Godsontmoeting*, 3 ed., Bilthoven 1959 (French translation: *Le Christ, sacrament de la rencontre de Dieu*, Paris 1960; English translation: *Christ, the Sacrament of Encounter with God*, London 1963).

[2] "Tout sacrament est un événement salvifique; cet événement s'accomplit sous la médiation d'un signe-de-la-foi". J.-M. R. Tilliard, "Principes pour une catéchèse sacramentaire vraie", *Nouv. Rev. Théol.* 84 (1962), 1044-61. Quotation from p. 1044.

minority of Catholics, both clerical and lay, in England (I shall call them the "intelligentsia", a word, incidentally, which had its origin in the nineteenth-century Russian revolutionary movement) I realize that unless they are helped to think in some such way about the sacraments they are not likely to remain Catholics very long.

What I am trying to draw attention to here is the real but unhappy split in the whole of modern culture, including theology, between "intelligentsia" and "the others". Certainly this is not the only factor in a divergence of fundamental attitude as far as theology is concerned—a fact which has been harshly illuminated in the first sessions of the Second Vatican Council.[3] But it seems important to realize that just as, say, Picasso, Stravinsky and James Joyce still remain unassimilated, still a preserve for "intellectuals", more than fifty years after they began their creative work, so too in theology there seems to be a parallel between current movements and the incomprehension and indeed the enthusiasm which they sometimes meet. Perhaps there is one important difference; I am doubtful whether the classic theology, in the form this assumed after centuries of isolation from contemporary life, has or had much pastoral meaning, much power to nourish and sustain Christian life, even among "the others". However, it seems likely that the newer theology speaks in the first place only to those in the modern world who are exposed to the pressures of contemporary society and have developed in consequence characteristic styles of self-consciousness as human beings in a shifting and uncertain world, where the one certain fact seems to be that things are changing, that history is on the move.

For the purpose of the present paper it seemed worthwhile to draw explicit attention to this uncomfortable state of affairs, because we shall be concerned here, in however small a way, with an attempt to indicate a new theological perspective, a reorientation of our thinking about God and the world; and I should like to emphasize *both* that this is not merely a piece of free speculation but a serious attempt to deal with real problems,

[3] Cf. E. H. Schillebeeckx, *Vatican II—A Struggle of Minds*, Dublin 1963, 7-16, and his reflections on Evelyn Waugh's article in *The Spectator* of 23 November 1962 in *De Bazuin*, 16 March 1963.

and that I am fully aware that for the majority of Catholic people these problems themselves have not yet become real at least in the sense of not yet having become explicit. Whether the task of *missionary* expansion, either in the old Christendom or in the new, does not of necessity impose the obligation of acquiring an explicit consciousness of these problems, is a question which I cannot afford to pursue here. I hope that both those who are familiar with the line of thought followed and any one who may find it novel will forgive me this prolonged introduction.

1: THE PERSPECTIVE OF THE MYSTERION

In recent years a good deal of attention has been given to the Pauline notion of the *Mysterion*, especially as it occurs in the Epistles of the Captivity.[4] The study of the Qumran texts has intensified interest in this Pauline notion, since it provides one of the clearest instances of a biblical theme which has undergone parallel developments in the New Testament and in the writings of this presumably Essene sect.[5] There can be no question here of attempting to cover all this ground again; but on the basis of these studies it may be possible to indicate certain features of this Pauline notion which will allow us to make a formally theological use of it in our present context.

Coppens sums up the generally-accepted view of interpreters of Pauline thought under twelve heads.[6] Summarizing this account still further, as far as possible in his own words, we may say that in the strong religious sense the term *mysterion* refers to the secret *plan* of universal salvation; the *mysterion* at the level of the divine existence itself. A plan of salvation realized in Christ: the *mysterion* at the concrete level of the divine *history* of salvation. This salvation offered to all mankind by the message of the *Gospel* and by *faith* in it: the *mysterion* at the level of human

---

[4] See for instance J. Coppens, "Le 'mystère' dans la théologie paulinienne et ses parallèles qumrâniens", *Litterature et théologie pauliniennes, Recherches Bibliques V*, Bruges-Paris 1960, 142-65.

[5] P. Benoit, "Qumran et le Nouveau Testament", *New Test. Stud.* 7 (1960-61), 276-296; id. art. "Paul: Epîtres attribuées à s. Paul", *Dict. Bib. Suppl. VII*, coll. 157-70 (Colossians), coll. 195-211 (Ephesians).

[6] Art. cit. 142-4.

collaboration in the perfect realization of it. Thus we have three groups of expressions: *mysterion* of God, *mysterion* of Christ, *mysterion* of the Gospel, of faith, of religion. The Epistles of the Captivity modify the earlier usage in four ways: firstly, the (plural) mysteries of the Christian economy are as it were concentrated in the single mystery of Christ, regarded in his being, his epiphany, the riches which he pours forth and the way he opens up to God; secondly, the mystery is no longer primarily the eventual salvation of the Jews, or the calling of the Gentiles, or the miracle of the parousia, or the glory of final beatification in God, but all these are "recapitulated" in Christ; thirdly, the mystery is no longer reserved to a restricted category but all Christians are called to share in its revelation; fourthly, the knowledge of the mystery becomes the final goal of Christian experience.

This may seem to be saying a good deal; but we must emphasize certain elements of Coppens's summary and add others to it. For in its formal aspect, concerned less with the content of the *mysterion* than with its divine origin, the *mysterion* is a mystery of God's *will*, τὸ μυστήριον τοῦ Θελήματος τοῦ Θεοῦ (*Eph.* 1:9). It is remarkable how frequently, and with what different expressions, St Paul refers to God's will or good pleasure, or purpose, or counsel in *Eph.* 1:1-14. Again, Christ, the concrete embodiment of this purpose, determined upon before the foundation of the world, recapitulates all things, both in heaven and on earth; Christ is the "image of the invisible God, the first-born of all creation", in whom "all things in heaven or on earth were created"; "he is before all things, and all things are held together in him, and he is the head of the body, the Church" (*Col.* 1:15-18). Thus Christ has a cosmic role in the *mysterion* of God's eternal purpose, and the Church, his body, is the manifestation in history of this *mysterion* consummated and embodied in the glorified Christ.[7]

It may be helpful to stand back here from this inevitably condensed statement of Pauline themes themselves extremely dense, and provide a kind of extended commentary on them taken from

---

[7] Cf. H. Schlier, *Der Brief an die Epheser*, Düsseldorf 1958; id., essays XII, XX, XXI in *Die Zeit der Kirche*, Freiburg 1958.

the second part of Isaiah. Consider for instance the following typical passage (46:8-12):[8]

> Remember this and consider,
>   recall it to mind, you transgressors,
>   remember the former things of old;
> for I am God, and there is no other;
>   I am God, and there is none like me,
> declaring the end from the beginning
>   and from ancient times things not yet done,
> saying, "My counsel shall stand,
>   and I will accomplish my purpose",
> calling a bird of prey from the east,
>   the man of my counsel from a far country.
> I have spoken, and I will bring it to pass;
>   I have purposed, and I will do it.

The themes of counsel ('ēsâh) and purpose, better "good pleasure", εὐδοκία (hēphes), run through all these chapters.[9] The counsel and will of Yahweh span the times, and are efficaciously realized and manifested in history, the history of God's saving interventions, *Heilsgeschichte*, as in the references to Noah (54:9), Abraham (41:8; 51:2), Moses (48:21; the Exodus theme, e.g. 51:9-10), David (55:3), each of them, it should be noted, individual figures through which God's general saving purpose is effected. A culminating intervention is "anticipated", in both senses of the word:

> From this time forth I make you hear new things,
>   hidden things (nĕsurôt) which you have not known.
> They are created now, not long ago;
>   before today you have never heard of them (48:6-7).

The theme of hidden things appears several times: the Servant, for instance, is "hidden" in the shadow of Yahweh's hand (hehbî'ānî, 49:2), "hidden" in his "quiver" (histîrānî, ibid.), we

---

[8] The translations generally follow the Revised Standard Version.

[9] I am much tempted by Dupont-Sommer's suggestion that the name "Essene" is a Greek rendering of the community of the 'ēsâh: *Les écrits esséniens découverts près de la mer morte*, Paris 1960, 55-6 (E. tr.: *The Essene Writings from Qumran*, Oxford 1961).

may say, in his predestining purpose. Yahweh himself is called *Deus absconditus* ('ēl mistattēr) in a remarkable passage: "Truly, thou art a God who hidest thyself" (45:15).[10] The statement should be read as an *O altitudo*, exactly paralleling St Paul's exclamation in *Rom.* 11:33, where *Is.* 40:13 is immediately quoted; it is an expression of awe before God's transcendence as revealed precisely in the wonder of the entry of the Gentiles. Yahweh's ways are unfathomable:

> For my plans are not your plans,
>   neither are your ways my ways. Oracle of Yahweh.
> For as the heavens are higher than the earth,
>   so are my ways higher than your ways
>   and my plans than your plans (55:8-9).

The mysterious divine purpose is revealed as mysterious precisely by way of the manifest historical intervention, the calling of Cyrus, for example. By the very act of showing himself in history God is revealed as transcending history, as *Deus absconditus*. Yahweh's saving action in Israel with its cosmic repercussions is performed

> that men may see and know,
>   may consider and understand together,
> that the hand of the Lord has done this,
>   the Holy One of Israel has created it (41:20).

Israel is an organ of revelation. She is Yahweh's witness: "You are my witnesses, says the Lord, that you may know and believe me, and understand that I am He" ('anî hû), "Here I am", the transcendent one who speaks personally as an "I" to his people and *presents* himself to them (43:10 and frequently); this "people whom I formed for myself that they might declare my praise" (cf. the refrain "in praise of his glory", *Eph.* 1:6, 12, 14).

Whether the so-called Servant poems are by the same author as the rest of Deutero-Isaiah or not, it is possible to see in them a prolongation of prophetic reflection in response to the apparent failure of the divine purposes after the first return from exile. The

[10] Rejecting the emendation of the *Bible de Jérusalem*, which makes the statement part of the *Gentile* acknowledgement of Yahweh's uniqueness: "With thee, Israel, God is concealed".

prophet's self-questioning in this critical time reveals to him the figure of a charismatic leader who will in fact be, however unexpectedly, the "new thing" which Yahweh has devised:

> For that which has not been told them they shall see;
> And that which they have not heard they shall understand.
> Who has believed what we have heard?
> And to whom has the arm of the Lord been revealed?
> (52:15-53:1).

It was the will (hāphēs) of the Lord to bruise him, the will (hēphes) of the Lord will prosper in his hand (53:10). By becoming 'āsam for the people he will reveal and effect the saving purpose of Yahweh.

In the final poem of cosmic rejoicing, the fulfilment of Yahweh's purpose is to be a memorial (sēm), an everlasting sign ('ôth 'ôlām) of the achieved *presence* of the hidden God (55:13); the *word* of the Lord is the expression of a purpose (hēphes, 55:10-11).

One last element may be added to fill out the notion of *mysterion* which we are attempting to characterize here with the help of the Old Testament. In an altogether remarkable book[11] Father Louis Ligier studies among many other themes the meaning of the knowledge of good and evil which was forbidden to the first man (I, 173 s.). It is impossible fairly to summarize the detailed riches of his study; and I shall merely quote here his final conclusion:

> How then are we to understand the prohibition of the tree? It teaches us that man can only enjoy the garden and life if, in the submission of faith and obedience, he respects the wisdom which unites from above the order of morality and the order of the promise. Since knowledge has a nomic or ethical aspect, the prohibition means that it is forbidden to evade the obligations defined by the word of God, the commandments. But, because of its prophetic signification, the prohibition also proclaims that it is forbidden to anticipate God's gratuitous designs. . . . Man must accept two limitations before God. A humility of obedience. . . . A humility of faith before a future whose secret God reserves

[11] *Péché d'Adam et péché du monde*, I, Paris 1960; II, Paris 1961.

to himself: a faith open to God's supernatural initiative, a progressive faith which accepts the dispensation of Time (192).

We may I hope be allowed to say that this prophetic knowledge of God's providential dispensation, to which man could have access only by God's free gift, was a knowledge of the *mysterion*. It was only by God's free gift that the First Adam could know of the Second, the Last Adam.

The perspective of the *mysterion* which we have tried so inadequately to sketch is in its simplest terms that of a God who makes himself present to us by the free gift of himself, a gift the condition of which is our acceptance of it in obedience and faith: God with us, Immanuel. In the rest of Part One of this paper, we shall try to see how we may exploit this notion theologically: firstly, as a way of defining the object of faith; secondly, as indicating the relationship between God and time.

One of the great achievements of scholastic theology (I am thinking here primarily of St Thomas) was its elaboration of a metaphysics of knowledge and the exploitation of this metaphysics for theological analysis. The essential feature of this metaphysics of the act of knowing is its recognition of the active role of the mind in constituting its proper object. Knowledge is an objectification of the world by and for the mind. Upon this fundamental act of objectification there depends the further, increasingly subtilized, analysis of formal and material objects and so on. While in the classic philosophy since the middle ages epistemology lost its ontological character, and knowledge was set over against being instead of being regarded as a special kind of being, knowledge was still regarded as consisting primarily in the apprehension of objects. It must be confessed that it is only in comparatively recent times that in various ways we have come to recognize philosophically that our knowledge of each other cannot be adequately interpreted according to the subject-object schema, even when the act of knowing is treated ontologically, as in St Thomas. The fundamental point here is not so much that persons are not objects, for at least in St Thomas's thought nothing is an object till it is made so, by and for the mind; it is rather that persons objectify *themselves*, as it were, or better, that they make themselves *present* to each other. We are not *for* each other by a process of objectification which each party to an encounter carries out privately by himself; we are for each other, present to each other, by a total behaviour of both parties, each having himself *for* the other. It is important that only human beings have faces, properly speaking (domestic animals, dogs and horses particularly, have faces of a sort precisely by being assumed into a domestic, human economy); because our faces are the chief organs of our mutual presence to each other, the mobile and expressive project of our self-presentation. Again, only human beings wear clothes, another style of self-presentation. Or consider the apparently senseless gestures we make when talking to each other over the telephone; divine revelation is sometimes spoken of as though it were a oneway telephone conversation without gestures. It does not seem to me possible for the classic objectifying or abstractive account of knowledge to deal satisfactorily with this obvious and fundamental feature of our knowledge.

If this is conceded, it follows that we should re-examine the exploitation of the classic account of knowledge when it is used for the analysis of faith. The dangers of over-simplification here, particularly in a brief note, are considerable; it is easy to knock down an Aunt Sally of scholasticism. Banez, for instance, developing St Thomas's distinction between the object of faith *ex parte ipsius rei creditae* and *ex parte credentis* (*S. theol.*, II-II, 1, 2) into a distinction between the *ratio formalis ex parte rei* and a *ratio formalis sub qua,* can find confirmation for his interpretation of St. Thomas's *veritas prima* as a *testificatio Dei revelantis* in the text of 2 *Cor.* 4:6, "For it is the God who said, Let light shine out of darkness, who has shone in our hearts to give the light of the knowledge of the glory of God in the face of Christ". Banez writes:

> As if the apostle were saying, the author of nature himself is the author of grace, who has shone interiorly in our hearts and minds, so that we might be certain (for this is what is meant by "knowledge", *scientia*) that the glory of God, that is, the divine majesty is in Christ's humanity, which is not improperly called a "face", with regard to men, since he

appeared to us through his humanity. So it is as if the apostle were saying: Our reason for believing that Christ is God, is that we have received God's testimony interiorly, God himself illuminating our minds (In II-II, 1, 1; 6a conclusio).

Rather than dwell upon this attractive text, which may easily lead us into the opposite error of interpreting scholastic theology as a sort of disguised personalism,[12] we may consider the role of *testificatio, testimonium, Deus testis* in this account. Although St Thomas does not explicitly use the notion in his *Summa theologiae* treatment of the object of faith, he does so in the contemporary *de Spe* (art. 1) and of course in the *de Veritate* 14, 8. It has several advantages. It brings out the role of the Church in proposing the faith (*fides quae*) to the individual believer. Thus in the article concerned with the heretic and his failure to accept the infallible and divine rule of the Church's doctrine, we have the fine statement, "Formale autem obiectum fidei est veritas prima secundum quod manifestatur in Scripturis sacris et doctrinis Ecclesiae".[13] What is more, it establishes a continuity of ontological identity between this proposition of the object of faith by the Church and by God and Christ. Again, it rests on the Johannine and biblical notion of *martyria*, witness. And yet, if we pursue this notion in St Thomas's commentary on St John, we shall see that its really essential role, that of constituting an object of faith *ex parte rei creditae*, prior as it were to its appropriation as an object *ex parte credentis* by the individual believer, needs to be completed by an account of God's personal self-proposition or self-presentation, through Christ and the Church, to the personal response of the believer.

There is a particularly striking passage in St Thomas's commentary on St John which I hope will allow me to make this

---

[12] I agree with R. Aubert, *Le problème de l'acte de foi*, 3 ed., Louvain 1958, 622 when he criticizes J. Mouroux for this in his otherwise interesting *Je crois en Toi*, 2 ed., Paris 1954.

[13] *S. theol.* II-II, 5, 3. Cf. M. Seckler, art. "Glaube" in *Handbuch theologischer Grundbegrffe*, ed. Fries, I, Munich 1962: "Die Struktur des mittelalterlichen Glaubens ist sozial: Der einzelne machte sich in Glaube und Taufe zu eigen, was die glaubende Gemeinschaft der Kirche unangezweifelt darstellte" (536). We may note the practice in the later scholastics of inserting the equivalent of a treatise *de Ecclesia* as an appendix to the treatise *de Fide*.

point clearly, though it does not contain any of the *testimonium* words. Commenting on *John* 5:24, "He who hears my word and believes him who sent me, has eternal life", St Thomas distinguishes between the human word which introduces us to faith and God himself on whom faith rests (*introducitur, innititur*). St Thomas explains how Christ can say what he does by pointing out that through Christ's human word men are converted to the *Verbum Dei*. "For since Christ is the *Verbum Dei* it is plain that those who hear Christ hear the *Verbum Dei*, and consequently believe God. Hence 'He who hears my word', that is, hears me, the *Verbum Dei*, 'and believes him', that is, the Father, whose *Verbum* I am".[14] For the proper understanding of St Thomas's meaning here we must remember that "Verbum personaliter dicitur in divinis". The human word of Christ introduces us in faith to him personally, the Word, and through him to the Father. It is only because we want to bring out more explicitly what St Thomas is exploring here that we appeal to a phenomenology of personal encounter; for we want to manifest the connection between the human word and the Word of God. To do this properly we should have to examine the whole notion of the word as *signum conceptionis intellectus*; but it may be sufficient to say here that human language is an articulation of the total behaviour of the human person by which he makes himself present. Thus in Christ we find a self-presentation of the Father in the Son, in the human face, gesture and speech of the Son. The "witness" in St John's gospel, as well as the witness of the gospel itself, is to the *person of Jesus*, answering the question, "Who is Jesus?"[15] The difficulty about St Thomas's mode of expression is that *Jesus himself* seems to vanish. It seems to me that an objectifying or abstracting account of knowledge cannot adequately bring out the personal self-presentation of God in Christ which constitutes the *reality* of revelation in which the *word* of revelation

[14] *In Jo.* 5, lect. 4; cf. lect. 6 throughout. *In Jo.* 8, lect. 3: "Ad hoc ergo quod immediate ipsum divinum Verbum audiremus, carnem assumpsit, cuius organo locutus est nobis".
[15] So the Catholic exegete H. van den Bussche, *Het vierde evangelie. I. Het boek der tekens*, Tielt-den Haag 1959, 132. We should understand the Johannine Logos not as a *verbum mentis* but as Jesus himself as the definitive self-revelation of God in history: thus the *whole* Prologue is about the incarnate Word, 100-17.

has its source and ground: we need to unify Incarnation and Revelation for faith.[16]

It is important to remember here that the *mysterion* is a perspective which can be summed up in the simplicity of God with us, Immanuel: a *mysterion* of God, of Christ, of the Gospel. We may then say that faith is a response, a total response of our whole behaviour and having of ourselves *for*, to the self-presentation of God in Christ, *Deus-in-mysterio* (which includes then *Deus testis*). The face of Christ and the word of Christ in the Church are the project of God's self-presentation to us and for us: "Philip, he who has seen me, has seen the Father" (*John* 14:9). Thus the "objective" proposition of revelation in testimony is contained within the personal reality of God's self-presentation in Christ, such that the whole tangible Christian economy, including our own embodied gestures of faith and summed up in the humanity of Christ, is informed by the active presence of God revealing (Revelation is *closed* but it has not *ceased*). The unique, total "object" of faith is *Deus-in-mysterio*, God's face, the smile of his good pleasure; it is the presence of his face to vision that we wait for in hope and faith.

As will be apparent, one advantage of defining faith and its object in terms of God's self-presentation in Christ is that our own response of faith is seen as assumed into an economy, a dispensation of the times, which has its origin in the eternal saving counsel of God's *mysterion*, the *sacramentum voluntatis Dei*. Faith and its object both belong to an historical economy. We may appreciate this better if we consider briefly the relationship between God's eternity and our historical time.[17]

Once again, we shall adopt the procedure of interrogating a classic scholastic position and endeavouring to fill out its implications. We may note by way of preliminary that to call God "eternal" is strictly to follow the *via remotionis*, to say how God

---

[16] Personal being as being-for is most perfectly realized in the subsistent relations of the Trinity; the Incarnation may then be seen as the transposition into human terms of the *being-for* of the Son. Thus the compatibility of the categories of substance and relation arises at the order of human personality before it becomes problematic in the Trinity. Personal being is intrinsically communication. "As-sumption" corresponds to "ex-pression".

[17] I very much regret not having been able to make use here of the important book by J. Mouroux, *Le mystère du temps*, Paris 1962.

is *not*, that not being subject to change he is not measured by time; that his eternal *now* is to be understood as the unity of something always abiding without change, as opposed to the *now* of time, which is the measure of changing things, distinguishing its before and after by its passage. The negative determination of eternity is thereby seen as characterizing a plenary actuality of being.

In his commentary on Aristotle's *Physics* (IV, lect. 23), St Thomas deals with certain difficulties about the existence and the unity of time. The chief point of interest for our purposes is that the two questions are *distinguished*. As regards the existence of time St Thomas make it clear that for its full realization it is necessary that it should be actually measured by an apprehending mind, just as change itself, not having, as change, a stable being (*esse fixum*) in the world, can only be grasped as a unified whole by an apprehending mind. Certainly time has an "ontic" basis, in that the being of the physical world in process of change is dependent upon God and not on the apprehending and measuring mind; but in its proper reality time is "ontological", assumed into the structuring consciousness of the apprehending mind. As regards the unity of time, St Thomas is quite categorical in his assertion that the single basis of this unity is the uniform, regular circulation of the firmament; and that time is primarily the measure of this primary circulation:[18] day and night are the rhythm of the entire cosmic universe, including man.

But suppose we are no longer able to grant the existence of such a cosmic clock? I do not see that we can argue to its existence from the metaphysical necessity of the unity of time. For it is possible to establish the unity of time in a different way.

Unlike visual art, music seems never to have been given the benefit of serious philosophical attention;[19] and yet it seems likely to offer an appropriate way of investigating time. For instance, the notion of rhythm, as applied above to the alternation of day and night, is surely in its primary application an anthropological notion: a characteristic of the beating of drums and

[18] Cf. *S. theol.* I, 10, 6.
[19] But see the recent book by the Swiss conductor E. Ansermet, *Les fondements de la musique dans la conscience humaine*, Neuchatel 1961, where he employs Husserl's phenomenology to interpret the musical experience.

the stamping of feet, the dance. In his valuable Harvard lectures,[20] Hindemith makes use of St Augustine (especially the sixth book of the *de Musica*) and Boethius to draw attention to the activity of what he calls "coconstruction" required in the perception of music. This co-construction is the active transformation of what is heard into musical meaning by matching it with a known musical image. Perhaps Hindemith's terminology is a little unfortunate here if we take "image" in too static or visual a sense; but considering the case of someone without previous musical experience he speaks of a primordial musical experience, common both to the novice and to music itself, namely motion: the novice has at least his experience of his own organizing acts of motility which allows him to perceive music as meaningful. We may call this originating motility the existential *a priori* of musical meaning.

To say "a priori" is deliberately to invoke Kant, one aspect of whose "Copernican revolution" was his account of time as "nothing but the form of inner sense, that is of the intuition of ourselves and of our inner state".[21] In our own times a far more influential revolution has been the re-thinking of Kant by Heidegger.[22] The essential feature of this re-thinking is the emphasis on the ontological foundation of Kant's transcendental method. That is to say, what Kant states in epistemological (and ultimately psychological) terms, Heidegger re-states in terms of the existence characteristic of the human existent, the *Dasein*. Thus the Kantian "form of inner sense" may be seen as the active "temporalizing" characteristic of human existence, revealed in the ordering of human existence as before and after in the *now* of a purpose or project. Individual or community time is *historical* time, the active assumption of the world into the orientation of human purpose.

My suggestion here is that this musical ontology of time, provided that we continue to accept its ontic basis, offers a way of preserving the unity of time as the unified and ordered project of God's providential purpose. Just as God is locally present to all things by containing them within his conserving act, so too

---

[20] P. Hindemith, *The Composer's World*, Cambridge (U.S.A.) 1953, esp. 1-22.
[21] *Critique of Pure Reason*, trans. Kemp Smith, 77.
[22] See e.g. M. Heidegger, *Kant und das Problem der Metaphysik*, Bonn 1929.

he is sempiternally[23] present to them in the same act; present, for instance, by initiating and working within the free historical acts of man. If finally we say that this providential purpose is summed up in the *mysterion* of Christ, then we may say that human history is measured by the economy of saving and sacred history; and that in faith God presents himself sempiternally to and for us in Christ: "the Alpha and Omega, who is and was and who is to come" (*Apoc.* 1:8) presents himself to us in the Son of Man, the Living one, who is "the First and the Last who died and behold he is alive for evermore" (cf. *Apoc.* 1:17-18).

2. THE SACRAMENTS AS PARTICULAR REALIZATIONS OF THE MYSTERION

The purpose of an approach to the sacraments which may not unfairly be called *a tergo* has been to indicate a perspective in which they are not simply a special department of dogmatic theology or liturgy, but the paradigms, the typical and pregnant instances, of an entire economy of salvation.

If faith is the response of our total behaviour, our having of ourselves *for*, the *Deus-in-mysterio*, who presents himself *for* us in successive historical interventions culminating in the passion, death and resurrection of his Son and the bestowal of the Spirit of testimony, then all expressions of faith are in their different degrees sacramental, in the broad sense of symbolic embodiments of faith. Our response of faith itself is incorporated into the significant economy of salvation initiated by God in Christ. Clearly a whole range of human activities may be discerned which exhibit our faith more or less manifestly. Through the centuries a whole ritual idiom has taken shape, and taken varying shapes, in terms of which the Christian may spell out his life of faith in his waking and even in his sleeping hours, from the cradle to the grave. In any individual or in any society, there will be not only variations of idiom but also gaps and lacunae; and there is also

---

[23] "Sempiternal: enduring constantly and continually" (Oxford English Dictionary). As opposed to "eternal", "sempiternal" is precisely a name applied to God *ex tempore* (cf. *S. theol.* I, 13, 7); it is intended to bring out that aspect of God's eternity whereby he is present (*praesentialiter adest*) to all time. Cf. *Contra Gent.* I, 66.

the possibility of free invention, professions of faith which enlarge the conventional idiom creatively. In this wide range of human activities, the expressive gestures of faith which we call sacraments in the strict sense have a canonical role, in the most obvious sense of being strictly determined by legislative authority in the Church, and further, as so determined, serving to determine the essential expressions of the faith of the Church. Canon law and rubrics are not, in principle at least, impertinent intrusions upon the expression of our faith (in practice one may sometimes have a rather different impression); for the sacraments are expressions of faith in which the Church realizes her being as *congregatio fidelium* normatively, prescribing ritual actions as bearers and witnesses of a faith continuous with her own origins, acknowledging her Lord as the summary, concrete presence of God's eternal purpose of salvation, and renewing on earth her Lord's own intercession with the Father. As belonging to the present economy of salvation, sacramental expressions of faith will more or less explicitly display symbolically the temporal perspective of the *mysterion*; in the Last Days of the eschatological interim between the Ascension and the Parousia, the faith of the Church is remembrance and expectation, focused upon the Lord of the ages; for upon us the end of all the ages has come (1 *Cor.* 10:11).

And it is the faith of the Church that when she so realizes herself in a normative gesture of faith, her Lord himself presents himself to her actually and actively, not merely as the initiator of her faith and not merely as hearing her prayer, but as himself the actual fulfilment of the prayer, as himself enacting in the expression of faith the *mysterion* which it symbolically displays. The ritual gestures of the sacraments of the Church are indivisibly the expression of the faith of the Church and the expression, by assumption, of the actual presence of the *mysterion* of Christ. The believing Church in act becomes full of her own mystery and the organ of the Lord's presence. By realizing herself essentially in faith she realizes herself as the Body of the Lord.

It is as we should expect above all in the Eucharist that we may discover in its concrete unity the particularization of the perspective of the *mysterion*. In a gesture the significance of which is obscured by our present rubrics and the printing of the missal, the Lord presents himself to us in his separated Body and Blood. The demonstrative "this" is the verbal expression of a gesture of self-bestowal in the gift offered to those who share in the fellowship of the table: "Take, eat, this ...". The real, substantial presence in the gift is the pledge of the actual and active presence of the giver;[24] and both gift and giver are at the same time representations of the faith of the Church, embodied in minister and offering. In other sacraments the gift is embodied in the receiver by a like active presence of the giver, embodied as the actual being-for of the receiver to the giver, as an intensification or a vivification of his initial response of faith. Furthermore, as ritually enacted every sacrament is a celebration of "archetypes", of typical gestures whose ἀρχή and *principium* is the *mysterion* of God's sempiternal presence displayed in the life of Jesus and consummated in the Johannine *hora*, the hour of the passage to the Father. Just as the mystery cults, whose ritual idiom has been assumed into Christian worship, referred themselves not simply to past time but to a primordial time of source and beginnings, so Christian worship refers itself by an anamnesis to the primordial source which is the embodied *mysterion* of the risen Christ, *in illo tempore, in mysterio*.[25]

Those who are familiar with Father Karl Rahner's vigorous and original work, *Kirche und Sakramente*,[26] will have noticed that use has been made here of his notion of a sacrament as a *Selbstvollzug*, a self-realization, of the Church, but that whereas Father Rahner sees the Church primarily as *Ursakrament*, primordial sacrament, here the Church is seen primarily as *congregatio fidelium*. We stand here before two alternative emphases in ecclesiology of which the most prudent view would probably be that neither should be maintained at the expense of the other, even if each has to be maintained by a different tradition.

[24] On "actual presence" see J. Betz, *Die Eucharistie in der Zeit der griechischen Väter. I-1, Die Aktualpräsenz der Person und des Heilswerkes Jesu im Abendmahl*, Freiburg 1955; id., art. "Eucharistie" in *Lex. für Theol. und Kirche*, III, Freiburg 1959, col. 1142-57; id. art. "Eucharistie" in *Handbuch theol. Grundbegriffe*, I, Munich 1962, 336-55.

[25] Cf. M. Eliade, *The Myth of the Eternal Return*, London 1955; id., *Patterns in Comparative Religion*, London 1958. Also *Man and Time*, ed. J. Campbell, London 1958.

[26] Freiburg 1960 (E. tr. *The Church and the Sacraments*, London-Edinburgh 1963).

In our present context however Father Rahner's views are of importance inasmuch as they include an interpretation of the Catholic teaching that Jesus instituted the seven sacraments (*Denz* 844).

The great merit of this new approach to an old and vexing problem is that rather than try to adapt a classic scholastic theology to the great fund of historical information about the development of sacramental practice and theology only assembled after the classic theology had taken definitive shape, Father Rahner starts with his new principle that the Church is the primordial sacrament as the sign of the eschatological real-presence of the victorious purpose of God's grace definitively established on earth in Christ. Thus although it is in only two cases, baptism and the Eucharist, that we possess anything like "words of institution" of what we now generically call sacraments, the Church possessed an *a priori* principle, her own character as primordial sacrament, founded by Christ, which, while only acquiring explicit formulation in our own times, yet allowed her in fact to recognize in her realizations of her own essence what we now call sacraments. Thus to say that Christ instituted the sacraments is to say that Christ instituted the Church as primordial sacrament and implicitly those diverse basic acts of the Church which we call the seven sacraments.

It is impossible here to examine these views as closely as they deserve, especially since it would involve trespassing on the subject of a later paper, but some general observations may be made. Firstly, it seems that any criticism of the more conventional interpretation of the institution of the sacraments by Jesus on the basis of historical implausibility tells even more forcibly against the view that Jesus instituted the Church as primordial sacrament. For what we are concerned with here is not the *ontological* foundation of the Church in the mysteries of Christ's death and resurrection, but the institution of the structured community of the Church in accordance with the declared human will of Jesus.[27] Now the primary sources for our knowledge of Jesus's will in this matter include those scriptural texts which are ordinarily appealed to as indications of his will that there should

[27] Cf. M. Schmaus, *Katholische Dogmatik*, III-1, 5 ed., Munich 1958, 49-201.

be sacraments: the calling of the apostles, the institution of the Eucharist together with the command to renew it whereby according to Trent (*Denz* 938) the apostles were constituted priests of the New Testament, the command to baptize and so on. And it is of course to these texts and related ones (e.g. *Eph.* 5 for marriage) that Father Rahner makes appeal too. But he appeals to them as capable of yielding their full content only in the light of a basic *a priori*, so basic as not to have achieved explicit formulation until our own day in terms of the Church as primordial sacrament. And this brings us to our second observation, that it seems extremely odd that when we already have a *de fide* principle of interpretation of the scriptural texts, namely that Jesus instituted the seven sacraments, we should have recourse to yet another principle, not yet, at any rate, defined authoritatively by the Church, in order to interpret the *de fide* principle and the scriptural texts. Thus while entirely (and gratefully) granting Father Rahner's case for maintaining that historically Jesus only instituted most of the sacraments *in genere tantum*, it would seem sufficient to say that the *a priori* principle which governed the increasing insight of the Church into the nature of the sacraments was precisely the principle that Jesus instituted them: that is to say, that in those pregnant engagements of her faith which we call the sacraments, the Church became increasingly aware that she was both doing and encountering Jesus's human will as the human expression of the *mysterion* of God's eternal saving will, by analogy, then, with those engagements of her faith for which Jesus's command was explicitly given. For (and this is the third observation) any account of the sacraments in their role as organs of grace which depends primarily on the Church (as primordial sacrament) and not primarily on Christ (as primordial sacrament) seems to misplace the proper emphasis.

Thus on the view suggested here the principle that Jesus instituted the sacraments constitutes indivisibly both an historical and a soteriological principle. It is possible to grant that the historical institution was *in genere tantum* in the sense that the basic declarations of Christ's human will contained implicitly what the Church later unfolded as seven sacraments (though it seems a good deal easier than Father Rahner somewhat polemically maintains to suggest ways in which that significance was unfolded even in apostolic times); but the point insisted on here is that the historical institution was the expression of the saving human will of the Lord of the Church, and that the Church in celebrating the sacraments does and meets that will sempiternally concretized in Jesus glorified.

It will be convenient to draw together the themes of this paper by way of a quotation from an important book on baptism in St Paul by a modern Catholic exegete. He writes:

> The basic idea of sacramental dying with Christ etc. rests on St Paul's characteristic mode of thought, which unites what belongs to saving history (the Adam-Christ parallel) and what is pneumatic and supra-temporal (ἐν χριστῷ). This bridging of a gap which is both temporal and substantial was only possible for St Paul in the figure of Christ himself, who on the one hand remains for him always the historical Jesus and as such—in the context of saving history—the Messias, and on the other lives on through the times (not supra-temporally in the sense of timelessly) as the pneumatic Lord, till he returns again as the Christ of the parousia.[28]

God's self-presentation in history culminates in his self-presentation in the glorified Christ, the Lord of the Church. Faith, which is itself an expression of that self-presentation, is also a human response to it. In the sacraments, which are the paradigms and archetypes of this encounter, the embodiment of faith is indivisibly an embodiment of the Lord of the *mysterion*, either both substantially and actively as in the Eucharist, or only actively as in the other sacraments. By our obedience in faith to Christ's command "Do this" in the sacraments, we behold, as in a mirror, the glory of God on the face of Christ, being transformed into the same image from glory to glory by the Lord Spirit (cf. 1 *Cor.* 13:12; 2 *Cor.* 3:18; 4:6).

---

[28] R. Schnackenburg, *Das Heilsgeschehen bei der Taufe nach dem Apostel Paulus*, Munich 1950, 158.

The Church, Sacrament of Christ

KEVIN McNAMARA

ONE of the central themes in Catholic theology throughout the centuries is that Christ is present in the Church. In a sense Christ is the Church, and the Church is Christ. While it would be an exaggeration to say that this doctrine was lost sight of in the centuries following the Reformation, it is certainly true that it has come very much to the fore in the present century. One can justly speak of a re-discovery of the doctrine of the mystical identity of Christ and the Church.

Among the categories in which theologians have sought to express this intimate relationship of Christ to the Church the most recent to find favour is that of "sacrament". The notion is borrowed, not primarily from the theology of the sacraments, but from the theme, familiar to tradition since St Augustine, that Christ is the "mystery" or "sacrament" of God: "non est enim aliud Dei mysterium nisi Christus".[1] As Christ is the visible expression of God in human history, so the Church is the visible expression of Christ. The outward form of the Church is not merely a veil hiding Christ from view. For those with eyes to see it also makes him visible. In the external structure of the Church the incarnate and risen Christ is revealed, and at the same time

---

[1] St Augustine, *Epistle* 187, CSEL 57, IV, 113.

made present and accessible. This in brief is what is meant by saying that the Church is the sacrament of Christ. The term "sacrament" is here applied in the broad sense familiar to antiquity, and echoed by the Council of Trent when it says that a sacrament is "a symbol of a sacred thing, the outward form of invisible grace".[2] The concept of the Church as the basic Christian sacrament in this sense is not completely new to theology,[3] but it is only in very recent times that it has become a major theme in ecclesiology. It is associated especially with the German theologians Otto Semmelroth[4] and Karl Rahner,[5] and under the powerful influence of the latter may well find much support in proposals for a doctrinal decree on the Church at the Second Vatican Council. Recently too E. H. Schillebeeckx has expounded the doctrine of Christ's relation to the Church in terms of "sacrament".[6] The doctrine of seven sacraments, no more, no less, remains intact: for sacraments in the strict sense are actions of the Church, whereas here we are talking of the common ground or basis of these actions, which is the Church itself.

It will be clear that behind the extension of the notion of sacrament from Christ to the Church is the traditional doctrine that in the Church the Incarnation of Christ is mysteriously prolonged. As the human nature in Christ is the visible form of the Godhead, so in the Church, which extends the Incarnation through space and time, the visible structure is the symbol and embodiment of the life of grace within. Divine and human elements are not, of course, related to each other in exactly the same way in Christ and in the Church.[7] However, the parallel is sufficiently exact to enable us to see in the Church a continuation of God's characteristic way of bringing salvation to men, which finds its supreme expression in the Incarnation of his Son. In the words and actions of men, that is to say in and through human history, God reveals himself to men in an offer of friendship and salvation. In Christ

---

[2] Denzinger-Schönmetzer 1639.
[3] We find it, e.g., in Scheeben. See *The Mysteries of Christianity* (E. tr.), St Louis 1946, 561-6.
[4] *Die Kirche als Ursakrament*, Frankfurt 1953.
[5] *The Church and the Sacraments* (E. tr.), London-Edinburgh 1963.
[6] *Christus, Sakrament der Gottbegegnung* (German tr.), Mainz 1960.
[7] Cf. Y. Congar, "Dogme christologique et ecclésiologie" in A. Grillmeier-H. Bacht, *Das Konzil von Chalkedon* II, Würzburg 1954, 239-68.

God himself is present in personal union with a member of our race, through whose life and death our salvation is accomplished. In and through the Church individuals are given the opportunity of making this salvation their own. And the law of sacramental activity finds a new expression. The Church exists, develops and acts within the framework of human history. In it Christ continues to be present under visible and historical forms.

Before going on to draw out the implications of the idea that the Church is the sacrament of Christ, it may be useful to relate this concept to other familiar categories used to express the mystery of the Church. Most important amongst them is the biblical image of the Body of Christ. The Church, as we say today, is Christ's mystical body. It is in terms of this doctrine that the twentieth century has made that re-discovery of the presence of Christ in the Church to which I referred above. Pope Pius XII has said that to describe the true Church of Christ "there is no name more noble, none more excellent, none more divine than 'the mystical body of Jesus Christ'."[8] These words of the encyclical *Mystici Corporis* of 1943 and the doctrinal exposition which followed them have set the seal of approval on a view of the Church which has had a decisive influence on religious life in our time. It was with real enthusiasm that twentieth-century Christians welcomed the doctrine of the mystical body. For it showed them how to find Christ their Saviour in the Church and, in addition, gave them a vivid consciousness of their corporate unity in faith and love. It is scarcely necessary to remark that the view of the Church as Christ's sacrament is not intended to replace the doctrine of the mystical body, or even to challenge its unique value in any way. It is simply yet another way of looking at a mystery that cannot be adequately represented by any single category or figure, that has always new aspects to be grasped and expressed. Basic to the two ideas of Christ's body and Christ's sacrament is the presence of Christ in the Church in visible form. This idea is arrived at differently in each case, however, and is accompanied by different insights. Other insights still are to be found in the well-known images of the Church as Bride of Christ and People of God. Where the figure of the Church as Christ's

[8] *Mystici Corporis* (C.T.S. tr.), par. 13.

body emphasizes the identity of Christ with the Church, the visible and corporate life of the body and the sanctifying influence of Christ the head on all his members, the idea of the Church as bride expresses rather the distinction between the Church and Christ, their mutual love and fidelity and the Church as already sanctified, as adorned with grace and virtue, holy and immaculate. But here too the mystical identity of Christ and the Church is not altogether lost sight of. Bride and Bridegroom do not remain distinct from every point of view; rather are they united in "one flesh" that is, in the one corporate personality which is also the "whole Christ", the head and the members of the mystical body in their union of life and action.

The idea of the Church as the people of God highlights yet other aspects of the mystery. As the people of God, the Church appears as the successor of the Chosen People and the heir to their divine promises; as the assembly of those who are called together by God's initiative and have responded in faith to the divine summons; as the people of the Pasch or Passover, which is passing from the slavery of sin to the life of grace, journeying through history to the final goal which is corporate glory in the risen Christ, constantly struggling against sin, praying, suffering and hoping until the day of Christ's coming. In this perspective the identity of Christ with his Church remains in the background. The emphasis is on the external form of the Church, rather than on the Church as "mystery" or as "sacrament", as the visible, historical expression of God and his redeeming love. Yet even here there are echoes of this theme. For the people of God is the people joined to God in an unbreakable covenant, in an intimate alliance of fidelity and love. And this Covenant is achieved in its final form on the Cross, when Christ by his death brings forth the Church and unites it to himself as his body for all eternity.

It will be clear then that the notion of the Church as sacrament of Christ is perfectly in harmony with the more familiar descriptions of the Church and its relation to Christ. In saying that the Church is the visible sign which reveals Christ and makes him present in history as the source of God's redeeming love, we are stating something that is already contained, sometimes clearly, sometimes not so clearly in other forms of expression. But the sacramental point of view has its own special contribution to make. It can help us to see in a new light that intimate relationship between Christ and the Church of which Christians today are so keenly conscious.

To begin with, the idea of the Church as the sacrament of Christ emphasizes the importance of the visible element in the Church. There is a recurrent human tendency to seek God immediately in a direct encounter of spirit with spirit, to dispense with the intermediacy of visible and social signs. This is a false interpretation of worship of God "in spirit and in truth". It has deceived many religious souls throughout the history of Christianity. The Reformers in particular failed to guard against it sufficiently. They seriously undervalued the visible element, rejecting the divinely-instituted hierarchical priesthood, the sacrifice of the Mass and all but two sacraments: baptism and the Eucharist. They sought a direct encounter with God, in which visible signs served merely as stimuli to faith and reminders of God's love, not as efficacious means of grace. This denial of the objective validity of the sacramental rite was met by Trent's definition that the sacraments confer grace *ex opere operato*, a doctrine that has loomed so large in Catholic sacramental theology in the intervening period that other aspects have tended to be understressed. Today, however, Catholic theology seeks to return to a fuller understanding of the sacraments by placing more emphasis on their personal structure and the *ex opere operantis* element. This development, combined with new tendencies among Protestants, is helping to bring Catholic and Protestant teaching on the sacraments closer. As a consequence, the sacramental view of the Church should help towards mutual understanding in ecclesiology, by leading Protestants to a better appreciation of the unity of visible and invisible elements in the Catholic conception of the Church. Since this problem is central to the whole ecumenical debate, it is important that any new approach to it should be fully utilized.

It is not only among non-Catholics, however, that the sacramental view of the Church may be helpful in acquiring a true appreciation of the Church's unity. Among Catholics too one sometimes finds a tendency to dissociate the visible and invisible elements in the Church: by giving the soul of the Church a wider extension than the body, for example, or by drawing a too radical distinction between the Church as divinely-instituted means of grace on the one hand and as interior community of grace on the other. If the Church is seen as the sacrament of Christ, as giving us access to Christ through a visible reality which reveals him and makes him present, such tendencies will be more easily avoided. In this way too, perhaps, certain false attitudes in the domain of personal religious life can be guarded against: for example, an aversion to what is termed institutionalism in the Church, that is, to fixed outward forms; or a chronic dissatisfaction with the Church as it actually functions and is administered, which is tantamount to taking refuge in an ideal, not genuinely human Church; or, more simply, a failure to see Christ in the Christian by subjects in their relations with superiors, by superiors in their relations with their subjects, by all Christians in their relations with one another; or, again, the recurrent temptation to expect God's grace to act directly instead of in the context of prudent, realistic planning and energetic action.

A further aspect of the sacramental unity of visible and invisible elements in the Church is the necessity of the visible Church for salvation for all mankind. God has attached the grace of salvation to the visible society he has instituted, and to it alone. This arrangement of God should not be looked at primarily from a negative point of view, however, as excluding from salvation all who are not linked to the Church, but from the positive point of view, that is, as containing an offer of salvation to all men through the Church. For God wills that all men be saved, and Christ has died for all and is the head not merely of the Church but of the entire human race. At the present time particularly, when the world has become one to a degree hitherto unknown, and when a new spirit of universal charity is welling up within the Church, it is vitally important that the Church be seen as the Church of mankind, as the sacrament of Christ for the whole world, the *sacramentum mundi*, as some modern theologians are expressing it. Catholics must become more conscious of this in the first place, and they must help to make the world conscious

of it too. A growing spirit of solidarity with the world and its
destiny, bringing with it a more courageous and positive outlook,
has been one of the most striking features of the Church under
the leadership of Pope Pius XII and Pope John XXIII, culminating in the encyclical letter *Pacem in Terris*, addressed by
Pope John to all "men of goodwill" throughout the world. These
men of goodwill are no strangers to the Church; they belong to
her and she exists for them. For them too she is the sacrament of
Christ, for in following their conscience they are responding to
divine graces which are drawing them towards her. For this is
what is meant by the *votum Ecclesiae* which justifies outside the
visible boundaries of the Church. The grace of charity which,
according to the teaching of the Church, is not denied to the man
who faithfully follows his conscience, finds its normal expression
in real membership of the visible Church. For those living within
the visible Church, sharing in the corporate organized life of the
people of God is the divinely-willed expression, the translation
into concrete and social terms of the interior life of communion
with the blessed Trinity. Basically, the same is true of grace
outside the Church. Whether the individual realizes it or not, the
grace he possesses is straining after the Church, looking for its
true expression and full development within the city; it is seeking
its natural realization in the visible sacrament of Christ. Thus the
Church stands in organic continuity with the barely or not at all
discernible multitude of her children throughout the world. The
visible assembly of the faithful, as Karl Rahner puts it, are the
advance troops of the forces of the Lord; behind them stands a
vast multitude which, for all they can say, may be as numerous or
more numerous than they are themselves.[9] It is vital that Catholics
be conscious of their close association with this amorphous host
that follows after them. It is only with their aid that the forces of
good can exert their full influence in the world. Moreover, it is
the duty of Catholics to reveal to them by their lives the true
nature of the Church, to play the part that belongs to them in
the Church's role of revealing Christ to the world. The Church
is sacrament of Christ, the visible sign of his presence, only in

---

[9] K. Rahner, "Dogmatische Randbemerkungen zur 'Kirchenfrömmig-
keit' " in J. Daniélou-H. Vorgrimler, *Sentire Ecclesiam*, Freiburg 1961, 783 ff.

and through the actions and behaviour of its members. It follows that the outward sign, while it can never fail, may be more or less effective. It can reflect Christ more or less perfectly. In other words: from the point of view of those outside who experience within their hearts the grace of Christ drawing them to the Church, that the visible Church is the answer to that interior longing may be more or less evident. To a great extent it depends on us whether their religious life will have to struggle for survival against fearful odds in relative loneliness and isolation, unsupported by a firm social framework; or whether it will find fullness and security in the organized life of the mystical body.

There is more to be said about this obligation of the Church and its members to show the way to Christ. Apart altogether from the wider perspectives we have just been considering, it is essential that Catholics, and particularly the clergy, should always remember that the Church exists only for Christ and has no other purpose but to lead to him. To say that the Church is Christ's sacrament is to stress the effective instrumentality of the visible ministry in leading us to Christ; but it is equally to stress that this ministry has no other purpose, no *raison d'être* but to lead to Christ. The primary danger here, perhaps, is not that the Church and the ministry may be used for other purposes, as for example the buttressing of economic and social institutions that should be discarded, though this danger exists; but rather that, to some degree at least, the Church in its outward form be made an end in itself. The Church must never be allowed to appear in the eyes of the faithful, must never become in the minds of its ministers, an organization pure and simple, a vast administrative bureau dispensing, however efficiently, sacraments and teaching and rules of conduct. This danger is certainly real if only because administration—and I mean *efficient* administration—is so essential in the Church; or because our loyalty to the Church and our desire to see it accomplish its task as competently as possible expose us to the risk of seeing only the visible Church, and losing sight of Christ whose instrument it is and is meant to be. In so far as we may succumb to this danger, we are forgetting the true meaning of all genuine religion, and of the Christian religion especially: namely that it consists in an intimate communion with God, a

profound and personal filial relationship with our heavenly
Father. To seek this personal relationship in isolation and without
the aid of visible rites is to run counter to man's nature and to
court disaster. But we may not forget that this relationship is the
genuine heart of religion. We are not to imagine that the administration of the sacraments and the government of the faithful can
promote holiness otherwise than by bringing this relationship
about and enriching it. That would be to fall victim to a mechanical
conception of religion. In fact, the Church's pastoral ministry
exists simply and solely to serve the life of faith, to bring God and
the Christian together in knowledge and love.

It will be evident from what has been said that the true conception of the work of the Church lies between two extremes: a
mechanical or materialistic view of religion on the one hand,
and an individualist or one-sided spiritual view on the other. It
is perhaps worthwhile to look once again at this latter danger and
to observe how the sacramental idea of the Church can guard
against it. The outward sign through which we have access to
Christ has the form of a society or community. It follows that it is
precisely as members of a community that we achieve union with
Christ. Christianity thus deals a crushing blow to the human
tendency towards egoism. Certainly the Christian is not called
to sacrifice his personal development by becoming an anonymous
unit in a collectivity. He retains his unique worth as an individual
person, but he draws near to Christ and attains personal fulfilment
precisely as a member of the whole Christ. His union with Christ
is at the same time union with the corporate body of which Christ
is the head. The more completely he identifies himself with this
body and leaves behind all pre-occupation with himself, the more
Christ-like does he become. The filial relationship with the Father
in Christ is at the same time a fraternal relationship with Christ's
brethren.[10]

All that has been said so far may be summed up as follows:
the notion of the Church as sacrament of Christ demands that
we take the visible structure of the Church seriously, as something
willed and established by Christ; that we see it as the instrumental

---

[10] On this and the preceding paragraph see F. X. Arnold, *Grundsätzliches
und Geschichtliches zur Theologie der Seelsorge*, Freiburg 1949, 13-54.

means of grace, not merely for Christians but for all humanity; that we give full weight to its social character and the implications of this for the Christian life, but that despite all this we never lose sight of the fact that the whole purpose of the visible Church is to lead the individual to interior communion with God in faith and love.

One further point was referred to and its implications are worth developing briefly. The Church, we saw, as the continuation of the Incarnation, makes Christ present in and through human history. This is, in fact, a very relevant point at the present time since there hinges on it the whole question of *aggiornamento*, with which the Second Vatican Council has made us so familiar. *Aggiornamento* is indeed a vital law of the Church. Its dogmatic basis is to be found ultimately in the Incarnation. When the Son of God came on earth he not only assumed an individual human nature; he became incarnate at a particular time in history, in a particular nation and family, in a particular human culture. In this way he made himself fully accessible to those to whom he preached. But as head of all humanity Christ wills to become no less accessible to every race and class of men throughout time and space. This he achieves through the Church. While giving to the Church a fixed visible constitution, he willed that this should clothe itself in particular human cultures, that the Church should follow the example of St Paul, who became "a Jew to the Jews, a Greek to the Greeks", and that it should become fully at home in each succeeding age. It is clear that this programme involves a twofold law for the Church: a law of incarnation and of freedom. The Church must immerse herself in the social and cultural conditions of this place and time; and yet she cannot be permanently bound to these conditions, she must retain a certain elasticity, the power to adapt herself to new conditions, to draw to herself new cultures, moulding them in a Christian mould. Thus at one and the same time the Church herself develops as she unfolds her latent powers, and new generations and nations are brought to Christ. Without *aggiornamento* the Church cannot be faithful to the Incarnation, from which she takes her origin; she cannot fulfil her role in history as sacrament of Christ.[11]

[11] Cf. B. Häring, "Tradition und Anpassung im Licht des Geheimnisses der Inkarnation" in J. Betz-H. Fries, *Kirche und Ueberlieferung*, Freiburg 1960, 276 ff.

At this stage it is time to ask what is the precise relevance of all this to the seven sacraments, with which after all this Summer School is concerned. This much at least can be said immediately: what we have seen gives us an understanding of the background against which the sacraments are to be given and received. The better we understand the laws of the Church's activity in the world, the more fruitful will be our reception and administration of the sacraments. For they are the principal means of the Church's action.

It is necessary, however, to underline the full significance of this. It is not only that the Church uses the sacraments for its purposes. The sacraments are the Church itself in action in this particular place and time, and for this particular person. The Church has a stable and permanent existence, but it exists with increased intensity when it is in action, when it is actually accomplishing the work of redemption for which it was established. Now this work is accomplished above all in the Mass and the sacraments. In these privileged actions the Church is present in its greatest intensity. For it is bringing the fruits of Christ's passion directly and in the most effective possible way to those for whom they are ultimately intended: particular individuals or, in the Mass, particular local communities. Thus we understand why the Church's sacramental nature, which is reflected in all its activity, reaches its most intense expression in these seven actions. They are the sacraments in the full and proper sense; in them the Church manifests Christ most perfectly and makes him really present: substantially in the Eucharist, dynamically in the other sacraments, that is, in his efficacious power of prayer and sanctification.[12]

In the light of this we can better appreciate certain truths about the sacraments. As expressions of the Church we must apply to them the conclusions we have drawn from the Church's function as sacrament of Christ. The need for adaptation in the liturgy, for example, is but a particular application of the general law of *aggiornamento*. Again, the *ex opere operato* efficacy of the sacraments has its basis in the role of the Church's visible structure in the giving of grace. Those who, so to speak, use the Church as

[12] Cf. K. Rahner, *The Church and the Sacraments*, 22-4.

outward sign, that is, conform to the outward conditions of
Church membership, are assured that they are thereby interiorly
sanctified, provided they have the necessary dispositions. God
has attached his offer of grace infallibly and for all time to the
Church as outward sign. The significance of the seven sacraments
is that in them this promise is reduced to concrete terms for the
individual at certain critical stages in his spiritual development.
In the sacraments the promise is most perfectly fulfilled; the offer
of grace is infallibly present. If it is to be effective, however, the
recipient must do his part.[13]

It is precisely this part of the recipient that recalls another point
made earlier. We saw the Church exists only to promote interior
union with God in faith and love. We must not make the mistake
of thinking that people are automatically sanctified if to the
outward eye the Church is functioning more or less efficiently.
At least we must be aware of, and guard against the danger that
routine and slipshod administration or reception of the sacraments
may greatly reduce, or even completely obstruct their sanctifying
effect. It is true that the sacraments, of themselves or, as we say,
ex opere operato, bring about a union of faith and love between
Christ and the recipient. But for this a certain minimum disposition is required in the recipient, and the effect produced will
be in proportion to the disposition present. The final purpose of
the sacrament is in fact to raise to a new height, vitality and
strength the movements of faith and love which are already there.

There is yet another aspect of the sacraments about which
much can be learned by setting them in the context of the Church,
namely their social significance. The Church, we saw, sanctifies
us in and through our place in her corporate life. Now the
sacraments remind us effectively of our dependence on the
ecclesial community. We depend on the Church to give us the
sacraments. She authorizes their administration and is herself, in
the person of her minister, the cause of the grace which they
transmit; it is through the Church that Christ gives this grace.
All this is, perhaps, familiar enough to well-instructed Catholics.
What they may fail to realize, however, is that the recipient of the

[13] Cf. A.-M. Roguet, "Les sacrements en général" in *Initiation théologique*
IV, Paris 1961, 437 f.

sacrament, no less than the minister, is acting in the closest dependence on the whole Church. For the sacraments are essentially signs of faith, ritual professions of faith by the Church. In them the Church unites herself to the worship and prayers of Christ her head. Because Christ prays with the Church, the sacrament is an infallibly efficacious petition to the Father for the offer of grace to the recipient. It is because of this petition that the sanctifying action of God follows, through the instrumentality of Christ's human nature and of the Church. It is essential, however, for a fruitful sacrament that the recipient not only intend to receive the sacrament—a condition which suffices for validity —but also that he unite himself with the Church's faith, with her worshipping prayer. It is only by worshipping with the Church in faith that he can be sanctified. Here is a very important social aspect of the sacraments. We cannot receive them except in that faith which we receive from the Church: thus we are reminded that we can only go to Christ in the company of all those who share our faith in Christ. In some way they are all at our side when we receive a sacrament; not only by their faith but also by their prayers, supporting us in our need. From this viewpoint the individualist approach appears more inadequate than ever. Yet how few realize that the sacraments are intended as expressions of our common unity in faith and prayer and as occasions for strengthening it!

It is possible, however, to acquire an even deeper understanding of the social and ecclesial significance of the sacraments. It is not merely that the Church, the entire Church, is deeply involved in the action of each sacrament. This action is also for her a means of growth. In a way that varies from one sacrament to another, it enables her to develop, to become more fully herself. She impresses on the recipient of the sacrament a likeness to herself, thus drawing him closer to her. He belongs to her more completely and she is more fully herself in him. The application of this to the individual sacraments can only be indicated here. It is particularly clear for baptism, the first effect of which is to make one a member of the Church. The bestowal of grace is a secondary effect, in the sense that it follows through incorporation into the Church. Something similar happens in the sacrament of penance, as was strikingly expressed in the ancient penitential discipline. To a greater or lesser extent every sinner has withdrawn from the Church by his sin, has in some sense shut himself out from communion with her. In the sacrament of penance the Church expresses her readiness to receive him back again, and it is through this restoration to the Church that his sin is forgiven. The same general principle is verified in the Blessed Eucharist, the sacrament of the Church's unity. It is by making us more perfectly members of his one mystical body, which is the Church, that Christ unites us and conforms us to himself in our reception of the Eucharist. In confirmation and orders, too, the Christian is given in different degrees a sharing in the Church's mission. The confirmed Christian shares in her prophetic mission, in her witness to Christ before the world in the power of the Holy Spirit; the bishop, and in a subordinate way, the priest, shares in her authoritative mission, her function of representing Christ as priest, teacher and ruler. In each sacrament appropriate graces are given, but these follow from the new degree of incorporation into the Church which has taken place, and of which the sacramental character is the sign.

Matrimony too gives grace by drawing the parties into a closer union with the Church; their mutual union is taken up into the mysterious union of Christ and the Church and in this way becomes a source of union with Christ in love. In extreme unction, finally, the Christian in grave illness is united with the Church in its role as conqueror of suffering and death; he is assigned a special position in the Church, where he is the object of special care and fervent prayer, in order that he may overcome suffering and pass from death to life and that his union with the Church may be sealed for eternity.[14]

Thus by one and the same process the individual is made holy and the Church itself is fulfilled. Through the sacraments the Church, in and with her members, advances towards her final goal. Already they give us a share in the future glory, but in a hidden way. They point to the time of fulfilment, when their full effects will be made known. Then the Church will have no further need of sacramental signs, because Christ will be present openly and his rule will be fully established in the hearts of the

[14] K. Rahner op. cit. 76-117; Schillebeeckx op. cit. 156-81.

just. In the meantime the sacraments are the most striking and effective expressions of God's love and of his purpose to give man a share in his own glory. From this point of view also they reveal the significance and purpose of the Church itself. For the Church is the abiding proof and instrument of God's definitive commitment of himself to man's salvation. It is a perpetual reminder that God is on man's side, that despite all appearances to the contrary, love has the final say in human destiny. In this sense too the Church is the sacrament of Christ. For it is in Christ that the Father has revealed himself and given us the irrevocable assurance of his love.[15]

[15] Cf. M. Schmaus, *Katholische Dogmatik* IV-1, Munich 1957 (5th ed.), 104-13.

The Sacraments and Our Lady

KEVIN O'DOHERTY

THE Church of Christ is continually guided by the Spirit of God. That the Church has survived crisis after crisis in the course of her history is sufficient proof that Christ's promise to send the Holy Spirit has been abundantly and effectively fulfilled.

But the assistance of the Holy Spirit is not confined to safeguarding the Church in times of danger and peril. The Holy Spirit is always present with the Church continually guiding her in the fulfilment of her divine mission: the sanctification and salvation of the human race.

It is not only in the light of past history that the influence of the Holy Spirit in the Church can be discerned. Those who see with the eyes of faith can find abundant evidence that the Holy Spirit guides and directs the modern Church as truly and as effectively as he guided the infant Church in the days of the first Pentecost. Evidence of this can be found in two great spiritual movements which have become prominent in this age of the Church and which, continuing to develop under the direction of the official Magisterium, will undoubtedly provide modern men with the most effective means for attaining sanctification and salvation. These are, of course, the Marian Movement and the Liturgical Movement.

These terms are used to describe developments in Marian and liturgical devotion which have had and continue to have profound and far-reaching effects on the spiritual life of the whole Church. These movements have influenced the practical exercise of piety precisely because they have revitalized the theology of the Church. The Marian and Liturgical Movements are predominant aspects of what is, in reality, a complete re-thinking out of the Christian message in terms of the realities of present-day life.

Theologians[1] have noted that these two spiritual movements seem to be opposed to each other. Liturgical piety is objective and sacramental; Marian piety is subjective and personal. Liturgical piety is governed by the principle "to the Father through Christ"; Marian piety has for its fundamental principle "to Jesus through Mary". Liturgical piety stresses the importance of the Christian community and fosters a more intelligent and fruitful participation in the public worship of the Church. Marian piety seems rather to stress the importance of the individual and to foster a more intimate and more personal devotion to our Saviour, Jesus Christ.

These differences present a challenge to theologians. That both spiritual movements simultaneously flourish in the Church is due to the inspiration of the Holy Spirit. The theologian must show how they can be harmonized and hence most effectively used to make all men true followers of Christ. For a complete solution of all the problems involved we may have to await further theological development of Mary's relation to the Church. Nonetheless, the theology of both movements has sufficiently developed to enable us to realize their importance and to understand that each can and should be promoted without detriment to the other. That we as priests should make every effort to promote both liturgical piety and Marian piety is the general theme of this paper.

To develop this theme, we shall attempt to establish two propositions. First: that Catholic spirituality must necessarily include devotion to Mary. Second: that because of Mary's association with Christ in the realization and application of Redemption, she must influence the dispensation of those graces which members of the Church receive through the reception of

---

[1] S. Em. le cardinal Frings, "Le Concile et la pensée moderne", *Le documentation catholique*, 59 (1962), 255 ff.

the sacraments and through the offering of the sacrifice of the Mass. We believe that these propositions lead inevitably to the conclusion that both Marian devotion and liturgical devotion must be fostered in spite of any practical difficulties.

The discussion will be divided into three parts: (a) devotion to Our Lady, (b) the relationship between the sacraments and Our Lady, and (c) marian devotion and sacramental spirituality.

DEVOTION TO OUR LADY

Christian tradition has always recognized a close association between Mary and her divine Son. "The Sacred Writings", said Pope Pius XII, "set the revered Mother of God as it were before our very eyes as most intimately joined to her divine Son and as always sharing his lot".[2]

Special significance has always been attributed to Mary's presence at the foot of the Cross. As early as the second century, the Fathers spoke of her as the New Eve most intimately associated with the New Adam in that struggle with the infernal foe which finally resulted in a most complete victory over sin and death.[3] Pope Pius XII called her "the most noble associate of the Redeemer",[4] and speaking of her presence on Calvary, said: "as another Eve she offered him on Golgotha to the Eternal Father for all the children of Adam sin-stained by his fall, and her mother's rights and mother's love were included in that holocaust".[5]

Mary's association with Christ is a constant theme in divine revelation. A mere enumeration of incidents is in itself sufficient to justify the conclusion that because of this association Mary played a unique role in the history of salvation. Mary had an active part in the realization of the mystery of the Incarnation. She shared the thirty years of hidden life. She intervened at Cana to request the sign which inaugurated the public ministry, the miracle by which "his disciples believed in him". She was present

[2] Pope Pius XII, *The Dogma on the Assumption*, New York 1951, 19.
[3] Ibid. 20.
[4] Ibid. 20.
[5] Pope Pius XII, "Mystici Corporis Christi", *Catholic Mind*, 41 (1943), 43.

at Calvary when the redemptive sacrifice was offered, when the Church was born from the side of our Saviour on the Cross. She was present again at Pentecost when Christ manifested and proclaimed his Church. Lastly, Mary alone now shares the bodily resurrection of her Son. This is the final mark of their intimacy, a mutual sharing in this final sign that Christ's victory over sin and death is complete and perfect. "These indications are obviously of varying value, but their very number and convergence serve to impress on us Our Lady's closeness to Our Lord in his work of redemption".[6]

When discussing Mary's participation in our redemption, theologians dwell principally on Mary's role in the Incarnation and on the significance of her presence on Calvary.[7]

At the Incarnation, God called Our Lady to co-operate with him at the very outset of his redemptive plan. She dedicated herself unreservedly to the tremendous design of God and her unqualified consent embraced, at least implicitly, the redemptive sacrifice. She furnished the flesh whereby the Word became man and by virtue of this flesh God became not only man but priest and victim. Thus, from the very first moment of the Incarnation, the Saviour and his mother are joined in the closest union, in a partnership and grace which is already an indication of Mary's co-operation in the redemption.

This indication becomes more explicit when we examine the significance of Mary's presence on Calvary. The partnership contracted at the Incarnation and consolidated by thirty years of close union is now further strengthened. She suffers with her Son and this sympathy goes far beyond a mother's natural affection. It extends to the intentions for which Jesus suffers. Her sufferings are truly meritorious for, as Pope St Pius X teaches, she merited in equity what Our Lord merited in strict justice.

It is difficult to understand the precise nature of Mary's role on Calvary but theologians unanimously teach that Mary played a significant and unique role in the objective redemption. This fact in itself amply justifies the veneration accorded to Mary by the Church.

⁶ R. Laurentin, *Our Lady and the Mass* (E. tr.), Dublin 1959, 26.
⁷ R. Laurentin, op. cit., 29-34.

Mary, therefore, is both the Mother of Christ and his associate in the work of redemption. She has also a special relationship to the Church which Christ has established to continue his redemptive mission unto the end of time.

Pope Pius XII, in his encyclical letter *Mystici Corporis*, has described the foundation of the Church in the following manner: "The divine Redeemer began the building of the mystical temple of the Church when by his preaching he announced his precepts; he completed it when he hung glorified on the Cross; and he manifested and proclaimed it when he sent the Holy Spirit as Paraclete in visible form on his disciples".[8]

Towards the end of the same encyclical, the Pope treats briefly of the relationship between Mary and the Church. He speaks of Mary as playing an important part in each stage of the Church's foundation. She gave her consent for "a spiritual marriage between the Son of God and human nature". In a marvellous birth she brought him forth as the source of all supernatural life and presented him as Prophet, King and Priest to those who were first come of Jews and Gentiles to adore him. Her prayer in Cana of Galilee moved her divine Son to perform that miracle whereby "his disciples believed in him". As another Eve, she offered him on Golgotha to the Eternal Father. Her mother's rights and mother's love were included in the holocaust and thus through the added title of pain and glory she became spiritually the mother of all his members. Finally, through her powerful prayers she obtained the grace that the Spirit of our divine Redeemer should be bestowed through miraculous gifts on the newly-founded hierarchy on Pentecost.[9]

Mary, therefore, co-operated in all phases of the Church's foundation—in the period of preparation, in the moment of foundation and in the moment of manifestation and proclamation. Mary can, therefore, with justice be accorded the title "Mother of the Church".

Pope St Pius X had already taught that Mary's spiritual motherhood of the Church is rooted in the mystery of the Incarnation. In the encyclical letter *Ad diem illum*, he wrote:

[8] Pope Pius XII, "Mystici Corporis Christi", *Catholic Mind*, 41 (1943), 10.
[9] Ibid. 43.

In one and the same womb of his most chaste mother, Christ took to himself human flesh and at the same time added to it a spiritual body made up of all those who were to believe in him. Therefore Mary, while carrying the Saviour in her womb, may be said to have carried likewise all those whose life was contained in the Saviour's life. All of us, consequently, who are united to Christ ... have come forth from Mary's womb, like a body attached to its head.[10]

Commenting on this statement Fr Cyril Vollert writes:

This is a true maternity. When Mary consented to the Incarnation, she represented all mankind and spoke in the name of the whole human race. When she conceived Christ, she spiritually conceived all the faithful. Because she is the mother of Christ the head, she is the mother of the whole body. This is not a mere moral maternity but is a supernatural reality, for Christ's members form one mystical person with the individual Christ, Son of Mary, a situation which has no counterpart in the relationship between a natural society and its founder. Accordingly the Incarnation establishes a vital union between us and Christ, and consequently between Mary and the Church.[11]

Fr Vollert then proceeds to explain how this maternity begun at the Incarnation attained its full perfection on Calvary:

The maternity which thus has its inception in the Incarnation is the ontological reason why Mary's co-operation with the Redeemer on Calvary could be elevated by God to a true generation of members of the mystical body. Although she was already the mother of the faithful because she was the mother of Christ, she did not become our mother in the fullest sense except from the moment when she was present on Calvary. At that solemn hour Jesus made her the mother of St John, type of all the disciples whom Christ and his Father love. At a stroke, her maternity acquired a new dimension. United to her Son in the sacrifice, she received

[10] Encycl. *Ad diem illum*, A.S.S. 36 (1903-4), 452.
[11] J. B. Carol (Ed.), *Mariology*, II, Milwaukee 1957, 562.

from him her maternal mission with regard to the Christian community. This is the proper understanding of the words, "Woman, behold thy son". For the Beloved Disciple represented all those who, like him, lovingly adhere to the Saviour. From then on Mary is fully the mother of the whole Church.[12]

Theologians explore many other aspects of Mary's relation to the Church but, as Fr Vollert says: "the truth that is most securely anchored in the sources of revelation and most clearly defines the relations between Mary and the Church is the simple fact stated by Leo XIII, that the Blessed Virgin is the mother of the Church".[13] As such, this doctrine admirably suits our present purpose which is to demonstrate that devotion to Mary must ever find a place in Catholic spirituality.

This fact, indeed, has long been acknowledged by the faithful who in every need, both spiritual and temporal, have recourse to Mary's intercession. This seeking of every gift and grace through Mary testifies to a belief in the power of Mary's intercession and, at least implicitly, includes the belief that Mary is the dispensatrix of all graces. This teaching has been made explicit in the writings of the theologians and has been incorporated in the official magisterium of the Church. The doctrine is found stated repeatedly in the teaching of the sovereign pontiffs. Pope Pius VII called Mary "Dispensatrix of all graces".[14] Pope Pius IX has said: "God has committed to Mary the treasury of all good things, in order that everyone may know that through her are obtained every hope, every grace and all salvation. For this is his will, that we obtain everything through Mary".[15] Pope Leo XIII has written: "With equal truth can it be affirmed that, by the will of God, nothing of the immense treasury of every grace which the Lord has accumulated, comes to us except through Mary".[16]

So clearly is this doctrine taught in the ordinary magisterium that all theologians accept the fact that Mary is the dispensatrix

[12] Ibid. 562-3.
[13] Ibid. 560.
[14] Ibid. 429.
[15] Ibid. 429.
[16] Ibid. 429.

of all graces. Theological investigation is now centred on an explanation of the nature of this prerogative. Theologians agree: (a) that Our Lady exercises some true causality in the dispensation of every single grace; (b) that Mary's function as dispensatrix of all graces is exercised independently of any explicit appeal to her intercession; (c) that she exercises this function at least as a proximate moral cause. The principal theological reasons supporting these conclusions are Mary's knowledge of our spiritual needs, her maternal concern for our spiritual welfare and the power and efficacy of her intercession.

That every grace comes through Mary is well supported by sound and serious theological arguments. Hence Mary's association with the redemptive mission of her divine Son did not end on Calvary nor with the establishment of the Church. She remains ever associated with her Son in the application of the fruits of redemption. Until the end of time, she will continue to exercise a unique and significant role in the sanctification and salvation of souls.

The thesis of this first section may be stated as follows: Mary's divinely-appointed role in the economy of salvation is such that Catholic spirituality must necessarily include devotion to Mary.

To establish this thesis, three points of Marian theology have been presented: Mary's role in the objective redemption, Mary's fundamental relation to the Church and Mary's prerogative of being mediatrix and dispensatrix of all graces. Exposition of these doctrines has been relatively brief and attention has been centred on the teaching of the sovereign pontiffs. Consideration of disputed questions has been deliberately suppressed in an effort to establish conclusively that Marian devotion is not based on a multitude of complex theological opinions but is solidly founded on truths clearly taught in the sources of divine revelation.

These prerogatives indicate that from the very beginning Mary was intimately associated with the redemptive mission of Christ and that she continues to exercise an important influence in the sanctification and salvation of souls. Prerogatives which reveal her as associated with Christ in a unique and singular manner in the whole economy of redemption clearly imply that devotion to Mary must be an essential part of the living of a full Christian life. God's will is revealed to us in the arrangement of events by his divine providence. Since he has so intimately associated Mary with Christ in every phase of the redemption, it seems evident that he intends us also to associate Mary with Christ in our efforts to attain sanctification and ultimately eternal salvation.

THE SACRAMENTS AND OUR LADY

Since Mary plays such an important role in the communication of grace, it is logical to ask what is the relationship between the sacraments and Our Lady, for the seven sacraments are the principal channels of grace in the New Law, the chief means whereby grace is communicated to men.

In discussing Our Lady's relation to the sacraments, most theologians confine themselves to two questions. The first question is: did Mary receive any of the sacraments of the New Law? Fr Roguet's treatment of this question can be considered as representative of the general teaching of the theologians.[17] His stated purpose is to study "the exact position of Our Lady with regard to each of our seven sacraments". His conclusions are: (a) Mary did not receive the sacraments of baptism or confirmation but she did receive the graces which these sacraments impart. (b) Mary most probably received the sacrament of the Eucharist between Pentecost and her Assumption into heaven. (c) Mary had no need of the sacraments of penance and extreme unction. Hence she did not receive these sacraments nor the graces which are their proper effect. (d) Mary "gathered into herself all the deepest beauties of matrimony". This conclusion is based on the significance of Mary's presence at the wedding of Cana, on the fact that she herself lived the mystery of the married life, and on the fact that matrimony is a symbol of the union of Christ with his Church and with each individual soul. (e) Mary did not receive the sacrament of order and was not a priest in any proper sense of the term. Nonetheless we can say "that she is in a way all

[17] A.-M. Roguet, O.P., *The Sacraments* (E. tr.), London 1954, 151-3.

around and above the whole priesthood". We can say so "because she is the type of the whole Church, at the same time virgin by her faith and mother by her charity, and because she took part so closely in the sacrifice of her Son".

Of the seven sacraments, then, Mary was incapable of receiving three: penance, extreme unction and order. Neither did she receive the spiritual effects proper to these sacraments. Mary did not receive the sacraments of baptism, confirmation and matrimony. But because of her plenitude of grace, she enjoyed in abundance the spiritual gifts and graces which are the effect of these sacraments. Finally, it is reasonable to assume that after Pentecost she received the sacrament of the Eucharist.

Fr Roguet's exposition contains some minor points with which other theologians might differ. One would particularly like to see a fuller exposition of his views on Mary's relation to the sacraments of matrimony and order. But he does accomplish his stated purpose of giving the exact position of Our Lady with regard to each of our seven sacraments and his exposition would be acceptable to all theologians.

This teaching reveals the extent to which Mary participated in those graces now normally imparted through the sacraments. No connection, however, is established between the sacraments as instruments of grace and Mary as the dispensatrix of all graces.

This is the second question: whether the graces received through the *ex opere operato* efficacy of the sacraments can be attributed to the intercession of Mary. The explanation of the late Canon Smith is taken as representative of the general teaching. He writes:

> But what of the grace which we receive through the sacraments? Is it not the teaching of the Church that the sacraments produce grace in us *ex opere operato*, by an intrinsic efficacy which they possess as the Christ-ordained instruments of our sanctification? And yet this grace, too, we receive through Mary's intercession. Of course, it must not be imagined that the efficacy of the sacraments is made conditional on Mary's intervention; for if a sacrament is validly administered and duly and properly received nothing can prevent it from producing its effect on the soul. But we

cannot receive the grace unless the sacrament is administered; and it is Mary's intercession which ensures that the sacrament is available. Moreover, the valid administration of a sacrament calls for the due rite to be used, as well as the requisite intention in the minister; and Mary is at hand to see that these conditions are not lacking. Above all, the fruitful reception of the sacraments requires the necessary dispositions; and Mary's prayer obtains that we do not frustrate the sanctifying virtue that flows from the sacred side of her Son.[18]

In this explanation, Canon Smith effectively disposes of any opinion which would deny that Mary exercises an influence on the dispensation of sacramental graces. We owe to Mary's intercession all those many and varied external graces whereby the reception of the sacraments is made possible for us. Likewise we also owe to Mary's intercession those internal graces whereby we acquire the dispositions necessary to receive the sacraments worthily and fruitfully. Hence it is quite correct to consider the graces received through the sacraments as graces dispensed by Mary. The conclusion is reasonable, for to except those most important of all graces from the dispensation of Mary would greatly diminish Mary's role as the dispensatrix of all graces.

There is, then, no conflict between Mary's dispensation of grace and the *ex opere operato* efficacy of the sacraments. This is confirmed by considering Mary's relation to the sacraments in the light of the general doctrine of the Redemption.

The basic plan of Redemption is clear. We have been redeemed by Christ and Christ's redemptive mission is continued through the Church. We are sanctified through the Church and the Church performs her mission of sanctification principally through the offering of the Holy Sacrifice and the administration of the sacraments.

In a unique and singular manner, Mary is the associate of her divine Son in his redemptive mission. She is honoured as coredeemer because of her association with Christ in the objective redemption. As Mother of the Church because of her association

[18] G. Smith, *Mary's Part in Our Redemption*, New York 1954, 170.

with Christ in every phase of the establishment of the Church—preparation, foundation and manifestation—and because at the moment of the Church's foundation on Calvary, Christ proclaimed her the mother of all his members who compose that Church. As the dispensatrix of all graces, she continues to be associated with Christ and hence with the Church in the sanctification of men. It would seem to follow from this that between Mary and the means of sanctification used by the Church—the Mass and the sacraments—there must be a relation analogous to that of Christ with whom she is so intimately associated.

Christ transcends the sacramental system. He is the author of the sacraments. He is the source and reservoir of all graces. It is to Christ that Mary is directly related. With him she was associated in the redemptive work. Her prayer, her sufferings, her offering of her Son to the Eternal Father were graciously accepted and freely made part of the sublime sacrifice whereby the world was redeemed. Mary is associated with Christ, the source and reservoir of grace. The sacraments are the application of what was accomplished on Calvary; thus, the sacraments which are the sacraments of Christ and the Church can be seen to be in some way also the sacraments of Mary.

MARIAN DEVOTION AND SACRAMENTAL SPIRITUALITY

Catholic piety receives its inspiration and direction from Catholic dogma. Mary's singular role in the economy of salvation provides the doctrinal foundation for Marian devotion. The importance of the Mass and of the sacraments of the Church amply justifies emphasis on active participation in liturgical worship. These two forms of piety must be harmonized, both in theory and in practice, so that our people may use to fullest advantage the means of grace placed at their disposal.

These two spiritual movements can be harmonized. Both have arisen and developed in the Church under the guidance of the Holy Spirit. The possibility of contradiction is, therefore, excluded and, consequently, any apparent conflict in the realm of doctrine must be due to a misunderstanding of the nature of true devotion to Mary or of the nature of sacramental spirituality.

But that does not mean that the theologians have as yet succeeded in fully demonstrating the harmony which must exist between these two forms of devotion. How these two forms of piety complement one another and how each can contribute to the development of the other will not be clearly seen until theologians attain a more universal agreement on the precise nature of Mary's unique and singular co-operation in the objective Redemption; until theologians can develop more fully the doctrine of Mary's relation to the Church, especially by exploring the hidden depths of the concept of Mary as prototype and image of the Church.

Enough development has taken place to indicate that these two movements have much to contribute to each other. Theological investigations which tend to clarify their underlying unity will help both to develop more surely and more rapidly to the greater glory of God and with greater benefit to men.

Meanwhile the priest engaged in parochial activity with the responsibility of guiding the spiritual lives of his people will encounter many problems in the practical order. But these are difficulties which can be completely or, at least, partially solved so that the practical development of both liturgical piety and Marian piety need not await further development in theology. An analysis of the principal difficulties will reveal the best means for attaining harmony in the practical order.

Considerable difficulty will probably be experienced in introducing the practice of liturgical devotion. Unlike the Marian Movement, the Liturgical Movement did not arise spontaneously from the general body of the faithful. It had its beginnings in the monasteries of Belgium, Germany and France. From these cloisters it has spread in a remarkable manner to embrace the universal Church. To the ordinary faithful, however, it is something new and strange. Suitable instruction must be given in order that they may appreciate the significance and value of liturgical devotion.

Education is, therefore, the first consideration. Appreciation of the liturgy requires a certain minimum knowledge of many things with which the people are not familiar. Among other things, they must be given some understanding of the nature and use of symbols and they must be made aware of the practical spiritual value of the sacred books of the Old Testament so that they may have some appreciation of the relationship between the Old and the New Law.

Necessary also will be the explanation of certain concepts which have little or no practical meaning for most people today. There is a great deal of individuality in the ordinary person's spiritual life—a major preoccupation with the saving of one's own soul. Such a preoccupation is both commendable and necessary. But it so dominates ordinary spirituality that there is little sense of the importance of the Christian community as such. That we are the new chosen people of God means very little to most Christians. The practical consequence of this is a failure to appreciate the relative importance of public and private worship. Another result can be discerned in the very attenuated concept which most have of such a common and ordinary term as "sacrifice". This, in turn, may very well be the reason why so many find it hard to understand why active participation in the sacrifice of the Mass is considered so desirable. Unless these and similar concepts are explained, how can the people attach any real meaning to the statement that "the liturgy is the celebration of our one-ness in Christ, as expressed and realized by the eucharistic assembly?"

The difficulty of re-educating the people towards an appreciation of the liturgy can be exaggerated. The knowledge required need not be profound. Even a very elementary knowledge can provide a firm foundation for an active and fervent spiritual life. Furthermore, we should not underestimate the capacity of our people to respond to our teaching nor forget that the grace of God which strengthens the will also illuminates the mind. Nonetheless, it is a formidable task which will require hard work and patience.

Patience may prove to be very necessary, for there is evidence to indicate that some of our Catholic people are prepared to offer a quiet but firm passive resistance to our efforts. Our Catholic people seem to have an instinctive appreciation of the axiom: *nihil innovetur nisi quod est traditum*. They quickly reject novelties in faith and they do not take kindly to what appear to be novelties in devotion. Good Catholic people are understandably reluctant to abandon the devotions to which they have become accustomed and in which they have so often found strength and encouragement. One indication of this is the tendency of very many to avoid the Dialogue Mass so that, as they explain, they may say their prayers without distraction.

More pronounced evidence of this is found in an article by Mr Evelyn Waugh, the English novelist, recently published in *The Spectator*[19]. Mr Waugh does not profess to be a theologian. But he does claim to speak as the self-appointed representative of the majority of ordinary Catholics. One section of his article is devoted to liturgical change. There seems to be no change in liturgy which has been made or which is proposed to which Mr Waugh does not object. He objects because he believes that some of them hinder and none of them help the devotional life of the ordinary Catholic. Perhaps Mr Waugh fails to appreciate the spiritual significance of the Liturgical Movement. But his opinions cannot be lightly dismissed for that reason. What he says deserves our respectful and careful consideration. They are the views of a man who has a deep reverence for the Church and a sincere respect for the priests and bishops of the Church. There are other reasons why his objections should not be passed over lightly but, of all of them, the most important is this: it is very, very probable that he is expressing the reaction of a large section of the Catholic laity.

We should not, therefore, expect the development of liturgical devotion to be an easy task. There will be practical problems to be solved, difficulties to be encountered and overcome. Development of Marian devotion will be a much easier matter. As mentioned above, the Marian Movement has arisen spontaneously from the general body of the faithful and is the fruit of their veneration, love and confidence in Mary, the Mother of God. No great effort need be made to foster and encourage devotion to Mary, for this devotion is already well established. But priests have a duty to guide and direct this devotion so that it might not be marred by excessive sentimentality and disfigured by practices which border on superstition. Certain forms of devotion to Mary

[19] *The Spectator*, 23 November 1962.

have, at times, been criticized. In some instances, the criticism may have been justified. Fortunately abuses are rare, but the fact that they do occasionally occur should remind priests of their duty to guide and direct the devotional practices of the faithful.

The guidance of popular devotion to Mary is a delicate matter. It would be most unfortunate if efforts to develop true devotion should result in diminishing the high esteem which our people have for the Mother of God. It would be ironical if prayer to Mary were to become less frequent or less fervent in this age of the Church when we are privileged to have such a great knowledge of the glorious prerogatives accorded to Mary by God.

Very rarely will we be called on to correct serious abuses and it is most unlikely that any word or act of ours would diminish the intensity and fervour of popular devotion to Mary. The practical and pressing problem is to guide and direct the already well-established Marian devotion in such a way that it will contribute to the development of liturgical devotion. There are several ways in which this can be done.

When the Blessed Virgin is the subject of an instruction or sermon, place the emphasis on Mary's singular and unique role in the economy of salvation. Divine revelation does not depict Mary as standing apart by herself in glorious isolation. Mary is constantly set forth as associated with Christ, her divine Son; as associated with the Church established to continue the sublime mission of the Incarnation; and as associated with us, the members of Christ's mystical body, in our efforts to prove ourselves worthy of our divine vocation as children of God and heirs to the kingdom of heaven. These prerogatives of Mary can be effectively employed to remind our people that they are members of the mystical body of Christ and to impress upon them the obligation to honour Almighty God by participation in the public worship of the Church.

Special encouragement should be given to those pious exercises which tend to foster and develop the theme of Mary's association with Christ, the Church and ourselves. The Rosary, already so popular, is a good example of such a pious exercise. Meditation on the mysteries recalls Mary's intimate union with Christ in every significant moment of his earthly life and the part she played in the foundation and manifestation of the Church. Repeated recitation of the "Hail Mary" reminds us that she acted as our representative at the moment of the Incarnation and is at the same time an appeal to her all-powerful intercession. The Rosary has a further advantage. Our people rightly regard it as more efficacious when recited in common, for the Rosary is traditionally a family prayer. Through a simple development and adaptation of this thought, it can be taught that the liturgical service is our family prayer as members of Christ's Church.

It might also prove beneficial to limit public devotions to Mary to the liturgical feasts established by the Church. The liturgy is surely intended as a guide to the emphasis which the Church places on devotion to Mary. By following the pattern set by the Church, we can be more confident that we are developing a balanced and sound devotion. We need have no fear that this limitation on public devotion will result in any neglect of the Blessed Virgin, for there are only two months of the year, April and June, in which Mary is not explicitly commemorated in the liturgical feasts of the Church. Placing emphasis on the official feasts of the Church gives assurance that Marian doctrine will be presented in the manner most conducive to the spiritual welfare of souls.

Priests must equip themselves for the faithful discharge of their responsibility to guide the spiritual lives of their people. In most cases some serious study of the theological principles underlying the liturgical movement will be necessary. Some priests may at first feel that there is little profit to be derived from the writings of many of the theologians who most strongly advocate the revival or restoration of the liturgy. The theology of these writers (e.g. Jungmann, Bouyer, Congar, Rahner, Davis, etc.) is not presented in the old familiar pattern of the seminary textbook. It may seem like a "new" theology. But such reading will prove worthwhile, if we start with the conviction that these theologians have something valuable to say and that their works are well deserving of serious study.

The amount of time available for serious study is strictly limited, for other parochial duties cannot be neglected. Fortunately, there are official documents readily available which provide both the theological background and the practical directions necessary for the development of liturgical devotion. These are the encyclical letters of Pope Pius XII, *Mystici Corporis* and *Mediator Dei* and the more recent instruction *De musica sacra et liturgia.* The first two give a clear and concise exposition of the nature of the Church and the nature of the liturgy. The third gives precise directions for training the people towards fuller and more active participation in liturgical worship. These documents outline the fundamental points of doctrine in which the people should be instructed and provide a practical programme for the development of a spirit of liturgical piety.

The enthusiasm necessary for the successful accomplishment of any project will often fail to survive, if serious difficulties arise. The development of liturgical devotion and the harmonizing of Marian devotion with it will undoubtedly be accompanied by a full quota of problems and perplexities. When these occur, we cannot do better than have recourse to Mary. She will not fail us. It is the will of God that she intercede for us. It is the will of God that the graces we need be dispensed to us by her.

The Sacramental Character

THE Council of Trent, repeating the Decree for the Armenians,
defined in its seventh session that three sacraments, baptism,
confirmation and orders, impress on the soul a character, that is,
a spiritual and indelible mark.[1] But the Church has not pronounced further on this doctrine. It is therefore the task of
theology to investigate and explain what the sacramental character
is and how this doctrine is connected with the other dogmas of
the faith. The theological text-books can scarcely be said to have
accomplished this task and modern theology has been uncharac-
teristically slow in undertaking it. Yet tradition is clear that the
doctrine is an important one. Innocent III described the sacramental character as "the character of Christianity";[2] St Thomas
states that it is "the root of the spiritual life";[3] Scheeben writes
that "in the sacraments by which it is produced, it, i.e. the character, is the centre of their entire causality and significance, and
that in the others it is the basis and point of departure of their
whole activity".[4]

[1] *Denz.* 852; cf. 695.
[2] *Denz.* 411.
[3] *Radix vitae spiritualis* (*In IV Sent.*, d. 22, q. 2, a. 1, sol. 1).
[4] M. J. Scheeben, *The Mysteries of Christianity* (E. Tr.), New York 1946,
582.

This essay attempts to investigate and explain, not every question connected with the character, but the fundamental question of what the character is and what its theological significance is. It studies the teaching of Scripture and the witness of tradition, following the evolution of the doctrine down to modern times. In this way it is hoped that the Church's understanding of the doctrinal significance of the character will be revealed and the foundation laid for determining its pastoral significance and application.

SCRIPTURE

There is no direct reference to the sacramental character in Scripture. This, however, does not mean that the doctrine of the character is unbiblical. Like so many theological questions, it is not treated explicitly in the Bible, but, in the light of later discussion, one can see that it is implied in the Bible's theology. If one were to examine the broad lines of the New Testament's presentation of the significance of the Incarnation and redemption, one would see there definite implications for character theology. The doctrine of the character helps us to understand more fully the central Bible message of redemption in Christ. The doctrine has a definite biblical basis. However, this biblical basis can be seen only in the light of character theology, i.e. the Church's growing reflection on the doctrinal implications of certain sacraments. According as events forced her to recognize these implications, the Church evolved the theology of the sacramental character. The biblical basis and implications of character theology are therefore best revealed, not by an *a priori* study of Scripture, but by following the course of this doctrinal evolution.

This evolution begins in fact with a biblical term which, though it is not a direct reference to the character, has nevertheless important implications for the doctrine. This is the term "seal", the Greek σφράγις. The theology of the character starts with this term and it is necessary to give a brief explanation of its biblical background. The biblical writers borrowed the term from ordinary usage. It meant a mark and could have many purposes. It was the

mark one placed on one's property to show to whom it belonged
or that one was now taking possession of it. Sometimes its purpose
was to protect property from interference, a warning not to inter-
fere, as, for example, the seal on a letter. Sometimes it was an
authenticating mark, authenticating a document, for instance.
Sometimes again it referred to the mark placed on human beings
to show that different individuals formed a particular group,
pledged to render service to some master. Roman soldiers were
thus marked with the seal of the Emperor, slaves with the seal of
their master. The basic significance always seems to be to mark
something off as belonging to someone and being at his service.[5]

Such is the ordinary usage of the term. Now the biblical writers
speak of the seal of God (*Job* 9:7, 14:17, *Daniel* 9:24). By this
they are referring to God's mastery over his creatures and over
history; creation is his property, marked with his seal.[6] But in the
New Testament the symbolism of the seal receives a new value
when Christ is said to be sealed by God, his Father: "Do not
labour for the food which perishes, but for the food which endures
to eternal life, which the Son of man will give to you; for on him
has God the Father set his seal" (*John* 6:27). In other words,
because he has been *sealed* by God the Father, Christ is able to
dispense eternal life. In this text Christ's power to accomplish
redemption is attributed to his sealing by the Father. Later in the
Fourth Gospel, Our Lord states that he is the Son of God because
God has consecrated (ἡγίασεν) him and sent him into the world
(*John* 10:36). One can, I think, associate this consecration of Christ
as Son with his sealing by the Father, so that the sealing refers
both to the *power* given him to accomplish redemption and to his
consecration as Son.[7]

To clarify the meaning of these texts, it is perhaps necessary to
invoke the aid of theology. There is question here, I think, not
so much of Christ's divinity, but of his humanity. In theological
terms what the texts mean is: in the Incarnation God seals Christ's
humanity in that he consecrates it—i.e. gives it a dignity and a
status—as the humanity of the Word and makes it the human

---

[5] Cf. F. J. Dölger, *Sphragis, eine altchristliche Taufbezeichnung*, Paderborn
1911, 18-65.
[6] Cf. *Vocabulaire de Théologie Biblique*, Paris 1962, col. 1003.
[7] Cf. *Vocabulaire*, loc. cit.

instrument of redemption. When one remembers that the basic significance of sealing is to mark something as one's own, to take possession of it and commit it to one's service, these texts seem to say that God takes possession of Christ's humanity so as to make it an instrument of redemption and, by consecrating it in the hypostatic union, to make it participate in Christ's dignity of divine sonship.

Turning now to the writings of the Apostolic Church, we learn from St Paul and the Apocalypse that the Christian also, through the Holy Spirit, shares in this sealing of Christ.[8] "In Christ", writes St Paul in *Eph.* 1:13, "you have believed and were sealed with the promised Holy Spirit". Again in *Eph.* 4:30—"Do not grieve the Holy Spirit of God, in whom you were sealed for the day of redemption". In 2 *Cor.* 1:22 he writes: "It is God who has put his seal upon us and given us his spirit in our hearts as a guarantee". In the Apocalypse we have reference to God's sealing of his servants: "Then I saw another angel ascend from the rising of the sun, with the seal of the living God, and he called with a loud voice to the four angels who had been given power to harm earth and sea, saying: "Do not harm the earth or the sea or the trees, till we have sealed the servants of God upon their foreheads" (*Apoc.* 7:2-4). Finally, in *Apoc.* 9:4, we are told of the swarm of locusts who were to attack men, "but only those of mankind who have not the seal of God upon their foreheads".

The Christian, then, is sealed by God. He shares in some way in the sealing of Christ. God takes possession of the Christian people and marks them as his own, just as he once took possession of the Jewish people and made them his own people. Henceforth it will be the Christian people who will be the instrument of God's designs on earth. God endows them with the gifts they need for this task. His endowment is a participation in the sealing of Christ. Christ's status as Son is shared by the Christian people and through them his work as mediator is continued and extended in the world and in history. There can be no doubt, I think, that in

[8] Cf. *Vocabulaire*, loc. cit.

St Paul the seal is a reference to the sacrament of baptism.[9] It is through baptism, therefore, that the Christian first comes to share in the sealing of Christ. The seal is part of his Christian endowment.

Is there any hint in the New Testament of a distinction between the seal and grace? This naturally is not a question which biblical writers explicitly consider. But there are some indications. The fact, for example, that St Paul indiscriminately calls all Christians *sancti* suggests that he has in mind an objective sanctity deriving from one's status as a Christian and distinct from the subjective or moral sanctity of individuals. There is also the significant text: "Do not grieve the Holy Spirit of God, in whom you were sealed for the day of redemption" (*Eph.* 4:30). The seal acquired at baptism endures unto the parousia. Yet St Paul feels it necessary to warn the Ephesians not to distress the Holy Spirit in whom they are sealed. He seems, then, to envisage the possibility of sin co-existing with the seal.

The biblical doctrine of the seal, though it is much too general to be simply identified with the later theological notion of the character, is nevertheless a source of great significance for character theology. The seal refers to God's possession and mastery over his creation. In the New Testament it refers to his taking possession of human creatures and endowing them with status and power to accomplish his designs. This is primarily and pre-eminently true of the humanity of Christ. But Christ's sealing is extended to his followers through the sacrament of baptism. Thereby the Christian people become God's people, sharing in a limited way in Christ's consecration as Son of God and in his status as mediator. They become the instruments in Christ of God's plan of redemption.

THE FATHERS

Turning now to the Fathers, we find that the early patristic

---

[9] Cf. J. de la Potterie, "*L'Onction du chrétien par la foi*" Biblica, 40-1 (1959), 15-22; A. Benoit, *Le baptême chrétien au second siècle*, Paris 1953, 103-105; A. Plummer, *The Second Epistle of St Paul to the Corinthians*, ICC, Edinburgh 1951, 37-40.

teaching relevant to the character is again concentrated on the metaphor of the seal. As in the Bible, so also in the early Fathers, the seal cannot be simply equated with the character. The doctrine is still too general and awaits proper definition. But it is an important source for the theology of the character and for the development of doctrine which grew up around the term.

The Fathers use the seal terminology in a variety of ways.[10] The sign of the Cross, for example, was a seal. But our interest lies in the use of the seal in the sacramental context. Though there has been some discussion in recent years as to what sacrament the Fathers associated the seal, the conclusion of Dölger, who wrote the standard work on the question in 1906, still stands. According to Dölger, the seal was associated with baptism until the beginning of the third century; after that date it was also associated with confirmation.[11] The reason for this change is, I think, liturgical rather than doctrinal. Perhaps one can best sum up the position by saying that the seal was associated with Christian initiation and particularly with baptism. This had one important consequence—the theology of the seal, and therefore of the character, developed as part of the theology of baptism. This was to remain true right up to St Thomas.

In the sacramental order the term seal was applied both to the external sacramental rite and to the spiritual mark produced by the rite. Thus, the Pastor of Hermas, dating about A.D. 150, states bluntly: "The seal is the water".[12] Many other documents of the patristic era likewise identify the seal with the external ablution of baptism and later with the consignation and anointing of confirmation.[13] Indeed, with some of the Greek Fathers, σφράγις became another name for baptism. This identification of the seal and the external rite was to have a long history, and it reappears again in the early scholastic period when the character is sometimes defined as the external rite.

[10] Detailed treatment of the "seal" terminology, its use and significance, in the patristic era may be found in the following works: F. J. Dölger, op. cit.; J. Coppens, *L'Imposition des mains et les rites connexes dans le Nouveau Testament et dans l'Église ancienne*, Paris 1925; A. d'Alès, *Prima Lineamenta Tractatus Dogmatici de Baptismo et Confirmatione*, Paris 1927.

[11] F. J. Dölger, op. cit., 179-83.

[12] Simil. 9, n. 16; Lightfoot's *Apostolic Fathers*, London 1893, 371.

[13] Cf. Coppens, op. cit., 313-23.

But the Fathers also use the term *seal* to describe the spiritual
effect produced by the sacraments of baptism and confirmation.
Their explanations of this effect, however, vary very greatly and
are seldom precise. They make rich use of the variety of secular
meanings which the term had and thereby multiply the metaphors.
The seal is a sign which distinguishes the Christian from the non-
Christian, a sign whereby he can be recognized; it is a sign of
sanctity and divine sonship, a sign of consecration and configuration to Christ and the Trinity; it gives one a title to the
indwelling of God and the Holy Spirit; it is a source of protection
and a sign that one belongs to the Christian community.

Two basic ideas of the seal run through these explanations. The
seal is a sign and a transforming mark, i.e., a mark which transforms the soul. The idea of the seal as sign comes of course from
secular usage and is perfectly valid when the seal is identified with
the external sacramental rite. But when the seal is used to describe
the spiritual effect produced by the rite, then this notion of sign
is going to prove difficult for the theology of the seal and the
character. For a sign must be visible, yet how can a spiritual mark,
a mark on the soul, be visible, at least to men? Though later
theology will attempt many answers to this question, the most
acceptable and today the most common view is that the spiritual
mark is visible through its visible effects, that is, through membership of and status in the visible Church.

The idea of the seal as a transforming mark owes much to the
text of *Heb.* 1:3, where Christ is said to be the χαρακτήρ τῆς
ὑποστάσεως of God, i.e., the express image of the substance or
being of God. χαρακτήρ, which means the express reproduction
of an image, is really synonymous with seal. Under the influence
of this text, the Alexandrian Fathers especially (e.g. Clement,
Origen, Athanasius, Didymus, Cyril) speak of Christ and the
Holy Spirit as being themselves the seal of God. Then, in turn,
Christ and the Holy Spirit impress their own image on the soul.
Cyril of Alexandria in particular develops these ideas.[14] The seal
primarily refers to the Son's resemblance to the Father which
derives from his eternal generation and their identity of nature.

[14] *In Epist. II ad Cor.*, in 1, 21-2, PG 74, 921-4; *Thesaurus*, 34, PG 75, 609-12;
In Aggaeum, 20, in II, 24, PG 71, 1061.

The Father then marks us with this seal, which is the Son, and
the Son in turn impresses on us the seal of the Spirit. We are
therefore marked with the seal of God and the Trinity, not by
nature or substantially, but by participation in the divine sanctity.
We are configured to Christ and through him to the Trinity and
come to participate in their sanctity. This theology of Cyril and
the Alexandrians is obviously a development of biblical ideas.
Further, the seal is considered in its normal context where it
implies and involves the presence of grace. This approach obscures
the real distinction between the character and grace and gives a
certain vagueness to the early patristic doctrine of the seal considered as character theology. Only extraordinary events will force
the Fathers to consider the abnormal situation of the seal existing
in isolation from grace. Such events will confront St Augustine,
who will be the first to make clear this distinction on which
further developments of the theology of the character will depend.
To the question, therefore: did the Fathers before Augustine
make a clear distinction between the seal and grace? the answer
must be: they did not. They had not the same urgent need to
consider the question as Augustine had and they naturally tended
to treat of the seal in its normal setting as not only orientated
towards but actually involving grace. The distinction between the
seal and grace was not for them an explicit question and therefore
they gave no explicit answer. Nevertheless, as Fr Leeming says:
"not a single Father or ecclesiastical writer can be cited as clearly
stating that the seal can be lost, while many clearly state that
grace can be lost; many say explicitly that the seal is indestruct-
ible".[15] The fact is that if one compares the Fathers' treatment of
the seal and their treatment of grace, one can see that the distinction between them is implicit in their writings. It remained
for St Augustine to make this point clearly and emphatically.

St Augustine was the first to develop a systematic doctrine of
the character and his influence on later character theology is
paramount. His great contribution was his identification of seal
and character and his clear demonstration that the character is
a permanent reality distinct from grace. I am not going to trace
here the stages of his controversy with the Donatists where he

[15] B. Leeming, *Principles of Sacramental Theology*, London 1956.

establishes this latter point. I would simply remark that it is a point of capital importance essential for further progress in this field. Had not this point been clearly made, the scholastic doctrine of the character would have had great difficulty in getting under way and the confusion of the character and grace would long have remained an obstacle to theological progress. Writing against the Donatists, Augustine concentrated on the important distinction between the character and grace. He did not develop much further the patristic teaching on the nature of the character but merely repeated the ideas current before him. He strongly emphasized, however, that the character is a sign that one is consecrated to and belongs to Christ and a sign that one belongs to the Church.[16]

In summing up the patristic teaching relevant to the theology of the character, one notes that this teaching is built around the biblical metaphor of the seal. In patristic writing this term covers a wider area than the reality later known as the sacramental character. But when the Fathers speak of the seal in a sacramental context, and this is the usual context, they are generally referring to what we call the sacramental character. The sacraments with which the seal is usually associated are first baptism and then, from the middle of the third century on, baptism and confirmation. Sometimes the term refers to the external rite but more usually it refers to a spiritual effect produced by the rite. In explaining the meaning of this effect, the Fathers speak of it as a sign that one belongs to God and the Church. They also see it as a transforming mark in that it consecrates and configures the Christian to Christ and to the Trinity. They do not, however, treat explicitly of the relation between grace and the seal but tend to consider the seal in its normal context as united to and involving the presence of grace. It remained for St Augustine to show that the seal, or character as he called it, was a permanent spiritual reality, an indelible mark, distinct from grace.

---

[16] On Augustine's theology of the character, cf. J. Galot, *La Nature du Caractère Sacramentel*, Brussels 1956, 36-41.

THE SCHOLASTICS

Further progress in the theology of the character does not occur until the twelfth century. Then the scholastics begin more or less where St Augustine left off. The question of the character is once again discussed in the context of baptism. Unfortunately, Augustine had frequently used the term "sacramentum" as a synonym for "character". When the early scholastics came to define baptism, therefore, there was for a period a strong tendency to define it in terms of the enduring reality it effected, namely, the character. Gradually this matter was clarified and the relationship between the different parts of the sacrament, that is, between the external rite, the character and grace, was fixed. The final solution was greatly facilitated by the neat and very apt terminology invented by Hugo of Saint-Cher, namely, the distinction in a sacrament of the "sacramentum tantum", "res et sacramentum" and "res tantum".[17] The character was then seen clearly as an effect produced by the external rite, distinct from grace but acting as an intermediary between the rite and grace. It was a spiritual mark impressed on the soul by the rite and disposing it for grace.

Once this confusion of terminology had been settled, the numerous other questions concerning the character which the scholastics were eager to discuss could be tackled. Such questions were: the cause of the character; its relationship with grace; the seat of the character; the number of characters; the indelibility and especially the nature of the character. It is with this last fundamental question that this paper is mainly concerned. But it may be remarked in passing that there was some doubt for a period in the medieval era concerning the number of characters. It was finally concluded that three sacraments, baptism, confirmation and orders, conferred a character. But disagreement still continued as to whether this did or did not mean three specifically distinct characters, some holding, as some still hold, that the character of confirmation is not specifically distinct from that of baptism. Then, as now, however, that was the minority view and, I think, the incorrect view.

The scholastic discussion on the nature of the sacramental

[17] Hugo of Saint-Cher, apud Galot, op. cit., 87.

character comprised two questions: 1. What kind of reality is the character?; 2. What does it accomplish? The first question, as Cajetan was later to point out, is really a metaphysical question, but it is very fundamental. The second is properly theological. The scholastics approached the first question by attempting to place the character in one of Aristotle's categories of being.[18] Here there was general agreement that the only category to which the character could possibly belong was that of quality. But there were four kinds of quality: figure, passion, power, habit. On this question the medievals could not make up their minds. They merely agreed that the character could not be a power, a *potentia*. Their reason for excluding *potentia* from the field was that they considered this to be a quality exclusively of the natural order. They could not conceive a supernatural *potentia*. The objection, as St Thomas later showed, was a weak one. But the fact remains that no theologian before him regarded the character as a *potentia*. Each of the other three qualities had their advocates. Against each serious objections could be brought forward. The quality of figure belonged to material, quantified objects; a spiritual figure would seem to be a contradiction in terms. Passion belonged to the sensible order whereas there was general agreement that the character belonged to the intellectual. Habit was either good or bad, whereas the character, it was agreed, was morally indifferent. Yet, despite these obvious objections, theologians opted for one or other of these views and defended it as best they could.

The second and more interesting question on the nature of the character is: "What does it accomplish or effect?" Here the scholastics attempted to develop the ideas we have already seen in the Fathers and which have their source in the biblical doctrine of the seal. Like the Fathers, the Scholastics also see the character as a sign which distinguishes and a mark which transforms. It marks those who possess it as belonging to God and to Christ and distinguishes them from those not so marked. The recipients of the different character sacraments, i.e. the baptized, the confirmed and the ordained, are distinguished from one another

---

[18] Galot, op. cit., gives a detailed treatment of the scholastic theology of the character.

according to their status in the Church. After some hesitancy as to how a spiritual mark could be a sign, it was generally agreed that since this mark was produced by an external rite which was visible, this mark was visible in its cause and therefore could truly be a sign.

As regards the spiritual transformation which the character effected, the scholastics did not really advance much further than Cyril of Alexandria. This question was discussed on the basis of two definitions which were classical in scholastic theology. The first of these definitions was taken from the *De Ecclesiastica Hierarchia* of the Pseudo-Denys, a fifth-century work, probably of Syrian origin, which the medieval era accepted as that of Denys the Areopagite and revered accordingly. The text speaks of the seal as a symbol that the recipient has become a sharer of the divine heritage and a member of the ranks of the faithful—*communicantem divinorum partis et sanctae ordinationis.*[19] Now though the context here is that of baptism, the seal referred to is simply the sign of the Cross traced by the bishop on the candidate during baptism. It refers neither to the baptismal rite nor to the spiritual mark produced by the rite. The *sancta ordinatio* is not a reference to the sacrament of orders but to the ranks of the faithful.[20] The scholastics, however, were unaware of this correct interpretation. They took the seal to be a reference to the character, turned the reference to sharing in the divine heritage to signify admission into the assembly of the faithful effected by the baptismal character and saw in *ordinatio* a reference to orders. As reproduced by the Scholastics, therefore, the text reads: *caracter est signum sanctum communionis fidei* (baptism) *et sanctae ordinationis* (orders).[21] As Alexander of Hales pointed out, this definition left no room for the character of confirmation.[22] In the eyes of some writers this weakened its authority, but for others it merely reinforced their contention that confirmation did not confer a specifically distinct character. Later this text was to play

[19] Pseudo-Denys, *De Ecclesiastica Hierarchica*, 2, 2, PG 3, 398.
[20] Cf. Galot, op. cit., 34.
[21] Cf. Alexander of Hales, *Glossa in Sententias*, apud Galot, 95.
[22] *Glossa*, 1. 4, d. VI, n. 2, a; IV, 105 (ed. Quaracchi, Bibliotheca Franciscana Scholastica Medii Aevi, XV), apud G. J. Connolly, S.M., *Sacramental Character in Five Famous Medievals*, Rome 1963, 15—"non videri haec definitio conveniri dato in Confirmatione".

a strange but decisive role in the formation of St Thomas's theology of the sacramental character.

The other definition is known as the magistral definition and was invented by Alexander of Hales.[23] It states that the character configures those who receive it to the Trinity and distinguishes them from those not so configured.[24] But as to the meaning of this configuration, the scholastics are not very helpful. The existence of three characters leads them to posit three degrees of configuration according to one's *status fidei*, i.e. one's status in the Church.[25] The configuration is generally taken to mean a configuration to Christ and through Christ to the Trinity, but the meaning remains vague and obscure and the writers find it very difficult to keep this configuration distinct from that of grace.

Some interesting efforts were, however, made to explain the configuration of the character. Thus, William of Auvergne describes it as "a certain kind of sanctity", *sanctitas quaedam*.[26] This sanctity, he explains, is distinct from sanctifying grace and he compares it to the consecration of churches and sacred vessels, a consecration which makes them holy and which they retain despite profanation. Thus baptism effects a sanctity which is distinct from grace and which the Christian retains despite sin, a sanctity which stems from the fact that he is consecrated and appropriated by God through the indelible mark of the character.

St Bonaventure suggested that the configuration of the character to God effected by the character takes place through the imitation of a divine quality. This quality is not a moral quality but a *gratia gratis data*, a charism.[27] By imitating such a divine quality man is configured to God, made like him. This description of the character as a *gratia gratis data* was a really brilliant stroke

[23] Cf. Galot, op. cit., 97 ff.; Connolly, op. cit., 14-15.

[24] *Glossa*, 1. 4, d. IV, n. 6, 1: IV, 108, apud Connolly, op. cit., 15—"Character est figura intelligibilis configurans trinitatem creatam increatae, facta per verbum sacramentale fidei Trinitatis, ad discernendum fidelem in statu suo"; cf. Galot, 97. The term *trinitas creata* derives from St Augustine and refers to three powers of the soul—memory, intellect and will; cf. Connolly, op. cit., 17.

[25] On the meaning of the term "status fidei" cf. Connolly 18-19.

[26] "Sanctitas quaedam est (character) cuius exemplum et figura est sanctitas basilicarum consecratarum et vasorum"—*De Sacramento Baptismi*, ed. Venice 1591, p. 402, apud Galot, 63.

[27] *In Libros Sententiarum*, 1.4 (Opera Omnia IV, ed. Quaracchi 1889) d. vi, p. 1, art. unic., q. 2 ad 3, apud Galot, op. cit., 159.

on the part of Bonaventure and pointed the way to a clear distinction between the configuration effected by the character and
the assimilation to God wrought by grace, *gratia gratum faciens.*
But imitation was hardly the word to use for it. As St Albert pointed
out, imitation implies acts of virtue, whereas the character is not
a principle of virtuous acts.[28] The only assimilation to God based
on imitation is that of the life of grace. Yet the elements of a
solution gleam through this notion of Bonaventure's, though he
left it too vague and undeveloped to be really useful. His insight,
however, will come to fruition in St Thomas who, instead of
speaking of the character as an imitation of a divine quality, will
describe it as a participation in divine power.

ST THOMAS

It is St Thomas' achievement that he was the first to produce
a real synthesis of character-theology, a synthesis which the
majority of theologians since his time have accepted. The century
of theological discussion which preceded him had prepared the
way for him. But where others are general, he is precise, where
others are vague, he is clear. Whatever criticisms one may offer
of it, his teaching on the character remains a wonderful monument
to his genius.

St Thomas developed his theology of the character mainly in
two works which, incidentally, are the first and last works he
wrote. These are his *Commentary on the Sentences* of Peter
Lombard, written in 1256, and Book Three of the *Summa
Theologica*, written in 1272. The basis of his teaching on the
character lies in the answers he gave to the two questions we
posed on the nature of the character. To the first question: What
kind of reality is it?, St Thomas replied that it is a spiritual power,
potentia spiritualis.[29] He is thus the first theologian to describe the
character as a power. This assertion is the basis of his whole
character-theology and in it he found the key to many difficulties
which had beset and defeated his predecessors. He makes little

[28] *In IV sent.*, d. vi, a. 4, ad 10, 1, ed. Paris 1894, apud Galot, op. cit., 159.
[29] *In Sent.* IV, d. 4, q. 1, a. 1 (ed. F. Moos, Paris 1947, vol. 4, p. 150);
S. theol., III, q. 63, art. 2.

of the traditional objection that *potentia* means a power of the natural order. He simply points out that there are also powers of the spiritual order and that these too belong to the quality *potentia*.[30] This power St Thomas defines as an instrumental power, a participation in the power of Christ. Recipients of the character become ministers of Christ through the instrumental power conferred by the character.[31]

Having defined the character as a power, the second question on the nature of the character: What does it accomplish?, becomes for St Thomas: What kind of power is conferred, what does it enable its recipients to do? The answer to this question brings us to the heart of the Thomistic theology of the character. Now, on this question St Thomas' texts need to be very carefully considered. Many commentators seem to overlook a very important point here because the texts are not studied carefully enough. This is especially true where the texts of the *Commentary on the Sentences* are taken together with those of Book Three of the *Summa* without due regard to the fact that the whole of St Thomas' productive life falls between these two works. The *Summa* must always be contrasted with the *Commentary* and this method is particularly necessary in the case of character theology. For on this subject there appears to be a significant change of doctrine between the *Commentary* and the *Summa*. It is necessary, therefore, to examine first the texts of the *Commentary* and then to proceed to those of the *Summa*. The relevant texts occur both in St Thomas' study of the character in itself and also in his separate studies of the three character sacraments. The texts must speak for themselves and I give first the texts from the *Commentary on the Sentences*.

The Commentary on the Sentences (1256)

Having made the distinction within *potentia* of a passive power and an active power, St Thomas writes:

---

[30] *In sent.*, ibid.
[31] *In sent.*, ibid.; *S. theol.*, ibid.

in spiritualibus est potentia spiritualis quasi passiva per quam homo efficitur susceptivus spiritualium actionum. Et talis spiritualis potentia confertur in baptismo. Alia potentia est activa spiritualis ordinata ad sacramentorum dispensationem et *aliarum sacrarum hierarchicarum actionum* exercitum. Et haec potestas traditur in confirmatione et ordine, ut suis locis patebit.[32]

Again, he describes the power conferred by the character as:

quaedam potestas qua potest in actiones hierarchicas quae sunt ministrationes et receptiones sacramentorum et *aliorum quae ad fideles pertinent.*[33]

Again, the character is conferred:

ut possit (homo) exercere spirituales actiones fidelium.[34]

The character, he repeatedly writes, is given for two purposes:

ut recipiens configuratur ad communicandum divinis sacramentis et *actionibus sacris;*

elsewhere:

ad participationem sacramentorum et actionum *fidelium;*

and again:

pro communione in sacramentis fidei et *aliis actionibus quae fidelibus competunt.*[35]

According to these texts the instrumental power conferred by the character enables its recipients to act in two spheres—in the sphere of the sacraments and in the sphere of what St Thomas variously calls "sacred hierarchical actions", "sacred actions", "actions of the faithful", "actions which pertain to the faithful", "actions which belong to the faithful". He explains clearly what he means by the sphere of the sacraments. The instrumental power here means either the active power to administer sacraments

---

[32] *In sent.* IV, d. 4, q. 1, art. 4 ad 3 (Moos, p. 164).
[33] Ibid., art. 1, corp. (Moos, 151).
[34] Ibid., art. 1, ad 5 (Moos, 152).
[35] Ibid., art. 2, ad 1 (Moos, 154).

or the passive power to receive them, the first associated with orders, the second with baptism. St Thomas does not explain clearly what he means by the other sphere of action, which he clearly distinguishes from the sacramental sphere, beyond stating that it involves an active power. We can, however, argue as to his meaning.

In his treatment of the character, St Thomas explains that the passive power of receiving sacraments is given in baptism and the active power of administering sacraments and of performing other sacred hierarchical acts is given in orders and confirmation.[36] Now he associates the *potentia* of orders with the power of administering the sacraments.[37] Baptism, therefore, gives the passive power to receive sacraments, orders the active power to administer them. But what of confirmation? Is the *potentia* conferred by this sacrament associated with the sacramental sphere or the other sphere of sacred hierarchical actions? Since the effect of confirmation must be the result of this *potentia*, an exercise of this *potentia*, St Thomas' particular study of confirmation will answer this question. In so doing it will throw light on the nature of the other sacred actions which, in his study of the character in general, St Thomas distinguishes from sacramental acts.

Now the effect of confirmation, according to St Thomas, has nothing to do with the reception or administration of the sacraments. Confirmation, he says, enables the confirmed to publicly confess Christ.[38] The confirmed in publicly confessing Christ act as the instruments of Christ and the Holy Spirit and as ministers of the Church. Their action is an action of the Church, an ecclesial action. Here, then, in the confirmed's public profession of the faith, we have an example of those sacred hierarchical actions pertaining to the faithful which St Thomas distinguished from sacramental actions in his study of the character.

By sacred hierarchical actions, therefore, St Thomas appears

[36] Cf. n. 32.
[37] Ibid., d. 7, q. 2, art. 1, obj. 1 (Moos, 278)—"potentia activa, scilicet dispensandi sacramenta, ad ordinem pertinet".
[38] Cf. ibid., d. 7, q. 11, art. 1, ad 1, ad 2 (Moos, 280-1); d. 7, q. 11, art. 2 (Moos, 286-7). Cf. J. Latreille, "L'effet de la confirmation chez St Thomas d'Aquin", *Revue Thomiste* 57 (1957), 29-62; A. Adam, *Das Sakrament der Firmung nach Thomas von Aquin*, Freiburg-im-B. 1958, 70-6.

to mean actions of the Church, i.e. ecclesial actions where the faithful act as the instruments of Christ. Now ecclesial activity is simply the continuation in the Church of Christ's triple function of king, prophet and priest.[39] The faithful act as instruments of Christ in all these spheres; they share in and continue Christ's mission as king, prophet and priest. This means that besides sacramental actions, which pertain to priesthood, the faithful also perform regal and prophetic actions through sharing in Christ's regal and prophetic power. Such actions of the regal and prophetic order are ecclesial actions and it is these St Thomas has in mind when he speaks of "sacred hierarchical actions" pertaining to the faithful but distinct from their sacramental or priestly power.

According to the *Commentary on the Sentences*, therefore, the sacramental character confers an instrumental power to perform sacramental acts and also other sacred actions which pertain to the faithful. By sacramental acts St Thomas clearly means acts of liturgical priesthood, though he does not use this terminology in the *Commentary*. Similarly we can see that the other sacred actions pertaining to the faithful are acts of the regal and prophetic order, though again this terminology is not used. The public profession of faith by the confirmed is one example of this latter activity. Thus, the *potentia* of the character involves participation in Christ's triple function of king, priest and prophet.

Summa Theologica

Turning now to Book Three of the *Summa*, the following texts sum up the doctrine there expounded.

> Sacramenta novae legis characterem imprimunt inquantum per ea deputamur ad cultum Dei secundum ritum Christianae religionis. . . . Divinus autem cultus consistit vel in recipiendo aliqua divina, vel in tradendo aliis. Ad utrumque autem horum requiritur quaedam potentia: nam ad tradendum aliquid aliis, requiritur potentia activa; ad recipiendum

[39] Cf. E. H. Schillebeeckx, *Le Christ, Sacrement de la Rencontre de Dieu*, Paris 1960, 77-117, 192-210. (E. tr., *Christ the Sacrament of Encounter with God*, London 1963).

autem requiritur potentia passiva. Et ideo character importat quandam potentiam spiritualem ordinatam ad ea quae sunt divini cultus.[40]

Deputatur quisque fidelis ad recipiendum vel tradendum aliis ea quae pertinent ad cultum Dei. Et ad hoc proprie deputatur character sacramentalis. Totus autem ritus Christianae religionis derivatur a sacerdotio Christi. Et ideo manifestum est quod character sacramentalis specialiter est character Christi, cuius sacerdotio configurantur fideles secundum sacramentales characteres, qui nihil aliud sunt quam quaedam participationes sacerdotii Christi, ab ipso Christo derivatae.[41]

Character sacramentalis est quaedam participatio sacerdotii Christi in fidelibus eius: ut scilicet, sicut Christus habet plenam spiritualis sacerdotii potestatem, ita fideles ei configurentur in hoc quod participant aliquam spiritualem potestatem respectu sacramentorum et eorum quae pertinent ad divinum cultum.[42]

Ad agentes in sacramentis pertinet sacramentum ordinis: quia per hoc sacramentum deputantur homines ad sacramenta aliis tradenda. Sed ad recipientes pertinet sacramentum baptismi, per quod homo accipit potestatem recipiendi alia Ecclesiae sacramenta. . . . Ad idem etiam ordinatur quodammodo confirmatio: ut infra suo loco dicetur. Et ideo per haec tria sacramenta character imprimitur.[43]

Thus, in the *Summa*, St Thomas describes the sacramental character as a participation in the priesthood of Christ. It is a *deputatio ad cultum*, deputing and enabling the recipient to participate in the public worship of the Church. The whole *ritus* of the Christian religion is derived from the priesthood of Christ. One can participate in this *ritus* or *cultus* only if one participates in the priesthood of Christ. The sacramental character achieves this participation by conferring the power to worship as an instrument or minister of Christ. This power is concerned with

---

[40] *S. theol.*, III, q. 63, a. 2 corp.
[41] Ibid., a. 3, corp.
[42] Ibid., a. 5, corp.
[43] Ibid., a. 6, corp.

the sacraments and those things which pertain to divine worship.
It may be active or passive. The active power is the power to
administer sacraments and is conferred in orders; the passive
power is concerned with the reception of sacraments and is
conferred in baptism and confirmation. By receiving this power
we are made like to Christ, configured to Christ, as one who
shares in another's power is made like him, configured to him.
The sacramental character is the character of Christ. As such it
is both a sign which distinguishes and a mark which transforms.
It distinguishes its recipients as Christians from non-Christians
and distinguishes Christians among themselves according to the
degree of participation in Christ's priesthood which they have
received. It transforms the recipient in that it configures him to
Christ the Priest and permanently consecrates him for participation in divine worship as a minister of Christ.[44]

Now in comparing this doctrine of the *Summa* with that found
in the *Commentary on the Sentences*, one notices immediately the
prominence given to the notion of priesthood in the one whereas
the term is never mentioned in the other. Before proceeding
further, therefore, with an examination of the texts of the *Summa*,
we must decide what kind of priesthood St Thomas has in mind.

This priesthood is concerned with the *cultus Dei*, the worship
of God. It has sometimes been pointed out that elsewhere in St
Thomas *cultus* means worship of God in a general or broad sense,
i.e. any true worship of God, any exercise of the virtue of religion.
The priesthood referred to, therefore, it is sometimes suggested,
is priesthood in a broad sense, the priesthood of the Christian
life. This suggestion, however, seems totally unwarranted. In
the *Prima Secundae* of the *Summa*, when treating of ceremonial
precepts, St Thomas distinguishes clearly between *cultus interior*
and *cultus exterior*, internal worship and external worship. By
cultus exterior he means the external worship involved in religious
ceremonies, i.e. liturgical worship. Thus he writes:

> Ordinatur autem homo in Deum non solum per interiores
> actus mentis, qui sunt credere, sperare et amare; sed etiam

---

[44] These points are made *passim* throughout the six articles; cf. Question
63 of Book Three.

per quaedam exteriora opera, quibus homo divinam ser-
vitutem profitetur. Et ista opera dicuntur ad cultum Dei
pertinere. Qui quidem cultus ceremonia vocatur.[45]

Now, it is this *cultus exterior*, liturgical worship, which is
referred to in question 63 of Book Three of the *Summa*, i.e. the
question dealing with the sacramental character. The texts show
this quite clearly. Thus, *cultus* is identified with the *ritus Christianae
religionis*. It is said to consist in *recipiendo vel tradendo aliqua
divina aliis*, but the examples adduced of giving and receiving
divine things are all examples of giving and receiving sacraments. Finally, St Thomas on numerous occasions refers to this
cultus explicitly as *cultus exterior*. Thus, he writes:

Character ordinatur ad ea quae sunt divini cultus. Qui
quidem est quaedam fidei protestatio per *exteriora signa*.[46]

Again, in the third objection of article 5, he speaks of the
cultus exterior ad quem character ordinatur.[47] The character,
therefore, is ordained to exterior cult, that is, the public, liturgical
worship of the Church.[48] Hence, the priesthood St Thomas refers
to in the *Summa* and with which he associates the sacramental
character is the liturgical priesthood and not priesthood in any
general sense.

Meanwhile, one notices in the *Summa* that St Thomas omits
all reference to the other sacred hierarchical actions, which,
according to the doctrine of the *Commentary on the Sentences*,
the character enabled its recipients to perform. In the *Summa*
only sacramental acts are mentioned, that is, acts of receiving and
administering sacraments. The reason for the omission is that
St Thomas has now confined the character to the priestly sphere,
i.e., the liturgical and sacramental sphere. The character is a

---

[45] I-II, q. 99, a. 3, corp.

[46] III, q. 63, a. 4, ad 3.

[47] Cf. also the reply to this objection, which discusses the indelibility of
the character and its continuing existence in heaven: "quamvis post hanc
vitam non remaneat *cultus exterior*, remanet tamen finis illius cultus", III,
q. 63, art. 5 ad 3. Cf. Schillebeeckx, op. cit., 82, n. 1.

[48] In III, q. 63, art. I corp., St Thomas refers to *cultum Dei secundum ritum
Christianae vitae*, but the reference here must be interpreted in accordance
with the general usage of the term *cultus* in Question 63 and must not be
interpreted on its own.

participation in the liturgical priesthood of Christ. There is no room here for actions of a regal or prophetic nature. In the *Commentary* he had posed an objection that his notion of character allowed room for only two characters, one for the reception of sacraments, another for their administration.[49] There was no room for a third. In the *Commentary* he was able to answer that objection because he was able to appeal to regal and prophetic activity. He does not repeat this objection in the *Summa*. It would be very interesting to know how he would have answered it.

The teaching of the *Summa*, however, creates a problem regarding the character of confirmation. In the *Commentary*, St Thomas has classed confirmation with orders as conferring an active power.[50] In the *Summa* he classes it with baptism as conferring a passive power somehow (*quodammodo*) enabling the recipient to receive the sacraments.[51] He promises to explain what this means in his treatment of confirmation. In fact, however, he never returns to the point again. When discussing confirmation, he simply repeats the doctrine of the *Commentary*—confirmation enables the confirmed to publicly profess the faith *ex officio*.[52] There is no mention of any sacramental power conferred by the sacrament, nothing to suggest that it has a special priestly and liturgical effect. It does not confer any new power in the liturgical or sacramental sphere.

The character of confirmation thus presents an acute difficulty for the doctrine contained in the *Summa*. The character represents a participation in the priesthood of Christ and confers a liturgical or sacramental power. The effect of the character must likewise be a power of the liturgical and sacramental order. The public profession of faith *ex officio*, which is the effect of confirmation, is not an action of the liturgical order. Therefore, the doctrine of the character contained in the *Summa* does not account for the character of confirmation.

The reason for the difficulty regarding the character of confirmation is that St Thomas has now confined the character to

---

[49] *In sent. IV*, d. 7, q. 2, art. 1, obj. 1 (Moos, p. 278).
[50] Cf. n. 32.
[51] Cf. n. 43.
[52] *S. theol.*, III, q. 72, art. 5 ad 2.

the sphere of liturgical priesthood. This sphere seems too narrow for the sacramental character and the doctrine of the *Commentary on the Sentences*, which left room for regal and prophetic as well as priestly actions, seems, in this respect at least, much more satisfactory. Certainly St Thomas did a very great service in giving prominence and expression to the notion of the priesthood of Christ in connection with the sacramental character. But this notion cannot be extended to explain the whole character field. Moreover, the thomistic doctrine of the character would lose none of its value if the teaching of the *Commentary* had been adhered to and the character seen as a participation in Christ's kingship and prophethood as well as liturgical priesthood. It would still remain an instrumental power configuring to Christ and demanding grace for its proper exercise and fulfilment. Modern writers sometimes try to avoid the difficulty by stating that the priesthood conferred by the character is priesthood in a general sense and therefore includes the regal and prophetic functions. Whether or not they are correct in this—and the contention raises difficulties of its own—this is not the priesthood St Thomas refers to in the *Summa*. He meant the liturgical sacramental priesthood and he adhered to this position despite the difficulty this concept posed for the character of confirmation and the inconsistency it appears to involve regarding this sacrament.

MODERN THEOLOGY

The theology of the sacramental character has received little development since St Thomas. But a fresh approach is apparent in some modern writers. Of these the two outstanding examples are M. J. Scheeben and E. H. Schillebeeckx. Though the approach of both these theologians is basically Thomistic, they are fully conversant with the theological history of the doctrine of the character. They therefore bring to the aid of the thomistic insight other traditional ideas which remained implicit and undeveloped in St Thomas' own writing.

Scheeben

Scheeben explains the doctrine of the character in close association with the doctrine of Christ and the Church.[53] Indeed, the character is the basic link between Christ and the Church, the reality which forms the Church and brings it into being. The Church is Christ living on in his followers; it comes into being through the formation of other Christs. In a way, it is the continuation and extension of the Incarnation. But to become other Christs, the members must share in the character by which the head becomes Christ. This participation is achieved by the sacramental character.

The character represents a certain participation in the hypostatic union whereby the second person of the Blessed Trinity became the God-Man, Jesus Christ. This union of the Word with Christ's humanity is the exemplar of the sacramental character. The assumption of a humanity by the Word gave that humanity a new dignity and status. It became the human nature of a divine person, capable of sharing in divine activity, a conjoined instrument of divinity. Scheeben calls this new and exalted dignity a consecration. Christ's humanity was *consecrated* the humanity of the Word. This consecration implies that Christ's humanity becomes a holy and sacred thing, endowed with the holiness of status; which is distinct from the holiness of grace. The natural result of this consecration was to produce grace in the human soul. In the case of Christ, this was an immediate effect of the union, since it was metaphysically impossible for any obstacle to grace to exist in Christ. The consecration of Christ's humanity was "the root from which the grace in his humanity sprang".[54] From it also stemmed his mediatorial powers of king, priest and prophet, which the work of redemption required. The hypostatic union, therefore, consecrates Christ's humanity as the humanity of the Word; establishes him in his human nature mediator between God

[54] Scheeben's doctrine on the sacramental character is found mainly in *The Mysteries of Christianity*, New York 1946, 582-92. The following exposition is based on these pages. Cf. also M. J. Scheeben, *Le Mystère de 'lÉglise et de ses Sacraments*. (Tr. A. Kerkvoorde), Paris 1956; B. Fraigneau-Julien, *L'Église et le Caractère Sacramentel selon M. J. Scheeben*, Paris 1958; F. S. Pancheri, *Il Pensiero Teologico di M. J. Scheeben e S. Tommaso*, Padua 1956.
[54] Scheeben, op. cit., 584.

and men; renders the humanity the conjoined instrument of divinity in the exercise of his mediatorial powers; and floods his soul with grace.

The sacramental character extends to men the consecration of Christ's humanity achieved by the hypostatic union. There can, of course, be no question of God again assuming a human nature by substantially uniting it to his own. God does not again assume a human nature. Rather, Christ reaches out and takes possession of man and man, once possessed by Christ, shares in a limited way in Christ's dignity as Son of God. By taking possession of him Christ joins man to himself in an organic union and makes him share in his own dignity and status. Man thus becomes in status an adopted brother of Jesus Christ and an adopted son of God. Organically united to the Head in Christ's mystical body, he becomes a member of Christ, another Christ, a Christian. He is a new branch grafted on to the heavenly vine. Christ accomplishes this union by taking possession of men and sealing them as his own. This seal is the sacramental character which marks men as belonging to Christ and reproduces in them the consecration and dignity enjoyed by Christ's humanity in the hypostatic union. Scheeben therefore defines the sacramental character as: the signature which makes known that the members of the God-man belong to their Head, which configures them to him and realizes their organic union with him.[55]

This configuration to Christ in the order of status should naturally involve configuration also in the order of life or grace. The divine life of the Head should flow to the members, the life of the vine should flow to the branches. Holiness of grace should follow holiness of consecration, we should be in nature what we are in status, other Christs. Grace springs from the character because the character brings us into organic contact with Christ, the source of grace, and gives us a right actually to possess grace. But men can set up impediments to the flow of grace. Yet even when they do, Christ does not revoke his action in sealing us and the continued existence of the seal "binds God's love so strongly to us that this love remains ever ready to give grace back to us even after we have trifled it away".

[55] Cf. Kerkvoorde, op. cit., p. 128.

Sharing in Christ's consecration as Son and mediator, Christians also share in the functions and activities which belong to Christ. They share in his regal, prophetic and priestly functions. Their consecration as other Christs confers on them the vocation, capacity and obligation to participate in these activities and thus continue the mediation of Christ. Christ's humanity was the conjoined instrument of his divinity in the exercise of these powers. Through the consecration of the character, Christians become his separated instruments for the same purpose. Thus is the work of Christ's mediation continued in the world through his members who form his body, the Church.

While Scheeben thus explicitly recognizes that regal and prophetic activity is just as valid an exercise of the power of the character as priestly action, he also insists that all this activity can be called priestly and that the character can be described as a participation in the priesthood of Christ. The reason for this is that Scheeben defines priesthood simply as mediatorship. Every form of mediation, even regal and prophetic activity, is therefore priestly. This means, however, that Scheeben uses two concepts of priesthood—the broad concept of mediatorship including the narrower concept of cultual priesthood.

Schillebeeckx

Schillebeeckx is one of the best-known exponents of the modern theology of the Church as the Sacrament of Christ. His writing on the sacramental character is naturally determined by this approach.

The impression of a mark in human society, he states, consists essentially in this, that it incorporates the person marked into a community placed under a competent authority, so that he receives officially an aptitude for action within and a mission towards that community.[56] The sacramental character is such a mark, giving one an aptitude and a mission within the community of the Church. Now the Church, being the extension of Christ in space and time, is, in its visible activity, like Christ, a sacrament,

[56] Schillebeeckx, op. cit., 189.

that is, a sign of grace charged with the reality it signifies. The visible activity of the Church signifies and confers grace. This visible activity of the Church continues the redemptive activity of Christ. It is therefore of three kinds, regal, prophetic and priestly. Every member of the Church, each according to his status, possesses these powers through participation in Christ's triple function. By exercising these powers the members create the visible activity of the Church and thereby continue the salvific work of Christ. The aptitude for this work and the mission to accomplish it are conferred by the sacramental character, which is a real consecration and configuration to Christ in his status as mediator.[57]

The activity of the character is called by Schillebeeckx visible ecclesial activity and it includes regal, prophetic and priestly actions. These actions compose the sacramental sign which is the Church and exhaust her visible activity. Every member shares in this activity according to his status in the Church. But, like Scheeben, Schillebeeckx also describes regal and prophetic activity as priestly and accepts the definition of the character as a participation in the priesthood of Christ.[58] The fact that he validly applies the term "sacrament" to a wider area than the traditional text-books envisage and can thus describe regal and prophetic activity as sacramental activity, certainly lends some justification to this usage. Yet one still feels that the term "priesthood" is being applied in two senses, since the definition of liturgical priesthood cannot be simply transferred to regal and prophetic activity.

CONCLUSION

In this review of the theology of the sacramental character one is struck by the consistency with which the same basic ideas keep recurring in the theology of different periods. These basic ideas may be summarized as follows.

The sacramental character is a sign, and a transforming mark;

[57] Cf. ibid. 193-208.
[58] Ibid. 201.

the sign bears witness to the transformation effected. This transformation refers to the change which takes place in a person when he is united to Christ. The theology of the seal and the character tries to express what this union with Christ means. Union with Christ implies configuration or assimilation to him; the person is made like Christ. But this assimilation is not the assimilation of grace but assimilation in status or dignity. We are made like to Christ in his status and dignity as Son of God and mediator between God and men. To understand the sacramental character, therefore, two things are necessary. First, we must understand what this dignity or status of Christ is; second, we must understand how men come to participate in it and what this participation means for them.

The action of sealing basically means to take possession of something, to mark it as one's own and to commit it to one's service. When God is said to have placed his seal on Jesus Christ, the reference is to the event of the Incarnation and hypostatic union. There God took possession of Christ's human nature and by substantially uniting it to his own made it the humanity of the Word. Thereby the humanity of Christ was marked as the humanity of God and was committed to the service of God as the conjoined instrument of his divinity among men on earth. The humanity of Christ thus came to share in Christ's dignity as Son and mediator and was enabled to play a vital part in his work of mediation.

The dignity bestowed on Christ's humanity in the hypostatic union is described by Christ himself as a consecration, a making holy. But, as the context in *John* 10:36 makes clear, the holiness referred to is not the holiness of grace, of likeness in the moral order of life. It is the holiness associated with a sacred dignity or status, such as, for example, the holiness of the Temple which the context shows Our Lord had in mind when uttering these words. This notion of consecration remains basic in the theology of the character in all periods and Scheeben is but re-echoing the witness of tradition when he makes it the basis of his theology.

The sacramental character extends the sealing and consecration of Christ to men. It signifies that Christ takes possession of men, unites them to himself in his status as Son and mediator and marks them as his own. It is thus that men become Christians, other Christs, and the seal bears witness to this transformation. The Christian is sealed as a son of God and mediator in and through Christ. He becomes the adopted brother of Christ and the adopted son of God: *Christianus alter Christus*. His union with Christ bestows upon the Christian his basic dignity, the dignity of being not merely a creature of God but a son of God in Christ. United to Christ, Christians form the body of Christ, the people and family of God. Their membership of that body and their participation in its life reveal the seal which marks forever their union with Christ and their Christian status.

Sharing in Christ's status as Son and mediator, the Christian receives from God a twofold vocation: he is called to the life of sonship and he is called, as an instrument of Christ, to the apostolate of mediation. He is called to transform himself in the likeness of Christ and he is called as an instrument of Christ to transform the world in Christ. He is given a personal and a social apostolate.

The assimilation to Christ effected by the sacramental character is an assimilation in the order of status, not of grace. But the assimilation of the character calls for and makes possible assimilation in the order of life, assimilation in grace. United to Christ as a member of his body, as a branch of the vine, the Christian is called upon to reform himself in the likeness of Christ. His union with Christ, the source of divine life, makes the attaining of that vocation possible. The impression of the character represents for the Christian a salvation event in which God addresses to him through Christ his saving word of love and mercy. The Christian must respond to that word and by responding merits for himself the favour of God, which is grace, and the divine assistance to lead a life in imitation of Christ, the life of Christian virtue. The character marks a covenant between God and man in Christ, whereby God makes man his son, a permanent object of his paternal love and mercy, and man pledges to God a life of filial obedience and love. The character continually calls upon man to fulfil that pledge and promises him God's assistance in the task. Assimilation to Christ in status is thus completed and perfected by assimilation in grace.

Sharing in Christ's status as mediator, the Christian is thereby called upon and enabled to share in and continue Christ's work of redemptive mediation. Christ's mediation consisted in the dispensing of word and sacrament through his regal, prophetic and priestly ministry. Upon his departure from this earth, he committed to his Church the task of continuing this mediation in the world and in history. The Church accomplishes this task through her members. They share in Christ's regal, prophetic and priestly power through the sacramental character. They therefore act as the separated instruments of Christ in dispensing word and sacrament. Every Christian, each according to the character he has received and his status in the Church, thus participates in the mediation of Christ and the Church and thus fulfils his social apostolate of building up the body of Christ.

Word and Sacrament

LOUIS BOUYER

Not many years ago it might have seemed that Word and Sacrament had become a divided heritage in a divided Christendom. The Protestant Churches boasted of being churches of the word, and in them the sacraments seemed to matter so little that they could be thought of as surviving organs from a dead past. The Catholic Church, on the other hand, appeared to the world as the sacramental church *par excellence*. In it, however, the word of God was not accented to the same degree, nor was the intimate connection between the word and the sacraments always clearly exhibited in thought and practice. For the Protestants the sacrament was nothing else but a kind of visible word, *verbum visibile* as the phrase is found already in St Augustine. But to them it meant only that the sacrament was simply an image, a material representation of what was better conveyed to us by the word itself, a kind of divine condescension to the grossness of our human and sinful nature just as parents express themselves in a childish way to make themselves better understood, but in a way that becomes unnecessary and even meaningless when the children are grown up.

Thus without realizing it the Protestants, while giving to the divine word and to the word alone full mastery over the Church life as a matter of principle, in fact betrayed a very impoverished notion of the word. They did not realize that a word which is so opposed to fact that it translates the momentous events of religious life into an abstract "meaning", is no longer the biblical word in its fullness and freshness.

On the other hand, the Catholics, by admitting at least implicitly that true sacramentality is something existing in itself and by itself as distinct from (if not opposed to) the word of God, prevented their sacraments from losing their reality and fading into a mere "idea" as occurred in the case of the Protestants. But they were running a great risk—that of conceiving or fancying that reality, thus divorced from the word and the intelligibility of the word was in a way more or less magical. To regard the sacrament as a kind of miracle, happening every time the right things are done by the right operator without any further consideration, differs very little from magic. This is a very good example of the risk which a theological teaching developing along a line purely or mainly polemical runs. It tends to distort itself by constant counterpoise with the error which it proposes to combat so that finally it may become nothing more than the said error seen in an inverted mirror. If—seeing that the Protestants have absorbed the sacramental reality into the pure meaning of the word—we divorce the sacrament from the word, we shall end not with the Catholic sacraments as they are in themselves, but with the Catholic sacraments as they are seen in the distorted vision of our opponents. Just when we congratulate ourselves on having repulsed the attack, the opposition has indeed conquered us as from inside. Here as everywhere Catholic truth cannot be understood solely as the contrary or negative of any error. Truth being a good is a plenitude; error being an evil is defective. We shall vanquish an error not by confining ourselves to the sole role of opponents but by re-establishing the true balance between this isolated aspect of truth (from which isolation the error has been born) and all other aspects, aspects which are not contradictory but complementary.

Just because the Protestants reduce the sacrament to the word the full Catholic doctrine on the sacraments cannot be expressed in terms that have nothing or very little to do with the divine word. Rather the word itself rightly understood means much more than the Protestants usually suspect so that its close connection with the sacraments, far from emptying them of their supernatural reality, is that which explains and constitutes them as God's great gift to man in Christ.

Our first problem then must be: what do we mean by the phrase "word of God"? People will tell you that it has many analogous meanings, meanings which must be clearly distinguished to avoid confusion. Thus, when we say that every pastor gives his parishioners the word of God in his Sunday homily, when we say that the Pope teaching *ex cathedra* pronounces the word of God, when we say the Bible is the word of God, and when we say Christ himself is the Word of God, we refer not to identical but to analogous realities. This is perfectly true—but there is something truer still. Those various realities denoted by the identical phrase "the word of God" are never to be seen in isolation. None of them can be properly understood except in and through its relation to all the others. For all together make an organic whole; apart from this connected unity each loses its full significance; the hierarchy which orders and connects them all is the first thing to be grasped.

The word of God therefore is not primarily a communication of some abstract ideas which God intends to bring to our knowledge as a professor of dogmatic theology instructs a class of students. If it were that, it would certainly have taken the form of a neatly composed handbook of scholastic theology, such as any theologian of the schools would be capable of producing for his pupils. But it is clear that the Bible falls very short of such an ideal manual. We may deplore this fact but we cannot help it! The only thing we can do, if we need some consolation, is to see what in truth the Bible is: how does the word of God present itself to us in its immediate embodiment in the Bible?

The divine word, as it has been committed once for all to the Church and as it discovers itself to us in the only text of which the author is God himself, is far more than a sum of revealed truths. It is first of all an act of God.

Let us notice here that every word still worthy of the name is something similar. Man himself has not originally spoken in order to compose lectures. Man speaks in order to assert himself, to intervene in the life of his fellowman and to modify it according to his will.

In the same way, as we see it in the Bible, God speaks to man to intervene in human affairs. More precisely, he speaks in order to take back as it were human life into his own creative hands.

Every human word which retains something of its primitive impulse and vitality is an intervention of man into the lives of other men. The same is true of the divine word in the fullest possible way. God has not spoken to Abraham to lecture to him on metaphysics, but to make of him the father of a new people who would become his chosen people, a people after his own heart. And from the first the *saying* of this fact has been so closely connected with the *doing* that the two can never be divorced. While speaking to Abraham and by speaking to him God remodels his life and heart. And, reciprocally, God speaks to Abraham in the events which occur through the divine agency no less than in visions, dreams or direct inspirations. All these experiences together express for him the word of God.

The same holds true for all the prophets. Why did the kings of Juda so eagerly want to suppress prophets like Isaias or Jeremias, who on God's behalf spoke unpleasant things to them? Because they were persuaded that the word spoken by the prophet as God's own word was not only stating what would happen independently of their announcement, but would produce it in a mysterious way. Of course, there was something here of a childish superstition, in that the kings and their people imagined they could suspend the course of events decided by God merely by suppressing his mouthpiece. But, on the other hand, it is perfectly clear that the prophets themselves were genuinely persuaded that God's word on their lips not only announced but determined the course of history in an infallible way—not because *they* spoke but because God spoke through them:

> Surely the Lord God does nothing (Amos says) without revealing his secret to his servants the prophets. The lion has roared, who will not fear?

> The Lord God has spoken; who can but prophesy? (3:7-8).

And again:

> For, behold, the Lord commands and the great house shall
> be smitten into fragments, and the little house into bits (6:11).

And the second Isaias will say in his turn:

> For as the rain and the snow come down from heaven, and
> return not thither but water the earth, making it bring forth
> and sprout giving seed to the sower and bread to the eater,
> so shall my word be that goes forth from my mouth; it shall
> not return to me empty but it shall accomplish that which I
> purpose, and prosper in the thing for which I sent it (*Is.*
> 55:10-11).

However, that power and reality inherent in the divine word
cannot be properly understood unless we appreciate its content
or object. As we have said already, this content is that the sons
of Abraham will become henceforth the sons of promise, the
People of God. It means that the word of God expresses first
of all a design, God's design on man, which is to be known through
its supernatural realization in the history of man, and which is
to be realized through being disclosed to man in a way that is
God's way to him. But the more the design is disclosed to those
concerned the more does the Designer himself come to the fore.
For the design of God for us, for his people, cannot be dissociated
from a revelation of God himself, since his design is to renew
his image in us. According to this image he created us in the
beginning, and he intends not only to renew it in spite of our sins,
but to bring it to an unspeakable perfection in the end. Therefore,
when with the history of Moses the design ceases to be a mere
promise for the future and begins to take shape in actuality, we
see going hand in hand with the revelation of the design of God
for us the revelation of the very nature of God, or rather—to use
the biblical term—the revelation of his name. On the Mount of
Horeb-Sinai, God wills to realize his covenant with his people
by showing them what they must become to be his in truth. This
is the revelation of the law, the revelation of the pattern to which
they are to conform. But before that, and leading up to that, on
the same mount in the burning bush God reveals his name to

Moses. And the connection between the two, this revelation of
the law as a first apprehension and realization of God's design
on man and the revelation of the unspeakable name of Yahweh
"He who is", will be so deeply felt that a *leit-motif* of the law will
be: "Be ye holy, as I am holy". Notice already that in the Gospel
in the new Sermon on the Mount the same connection will be
still more explicitly underlined by Our Lord himself. He will
reveal God fully as the Father, as him who loves with that
creative, redemptive love which is so typically his that St John
will use the equivalent "God is Love". But he will do that while
saying to his disciples: "Be perfect, as your heavenly Father is
perfect"—having made it clear that the perfection intended is
that of love, of God's own love.

Throughout the Bible, therefore, from beginning to end, that
communication which is God's word in its fundamental sense
will be both a communication of what we are to be and a communication of what he is, neither being separate from the other
since we are to become in some way like to him, and we cannot
discover in truth what he is except by becoming just that through
the gift of his grace. Therefore, for the pious Jew the law of God
will be nothing other than an impression upon his whole life and
being of the most holy name of God. Already for him the yoke
of the law, whatever its demands may be, will be an easy yoke
and a light burden.

In that intimate interconnection between the revelation of the
divine name and that of the design of God for us (it is impossible
to acknowledge the name in truth without being renewed by the
fulfilment in us of the design) we have a cue to what the Bible
means by the "knowledge of God", "to know God". To know
God, as his words intend to make us know him, is not only to
have right ideas about him. It is to be admitted into his intimacy,
to be made his own in reality, and therefore to conform to his
will, and even become mysteriously united to him in such a way
that his life becomes one with our own. Hence the very significant
use of "to know" in Hebrew to denote the union between man
and woman—this is corroborated by the image (indeed more
than an image) of God's espousals with his people as we find it
already in Osee and Ezekiel. To know God in the way in which

he is to be known through his word accepted in obedient faith is not only to comply with his will but to be conformed in our whole being to his being, by being made one with him through his wonderful grace.

What we have tried to sum up from the Old Testament has to be kept in mind when we come to the central truths of the New: that God's Word has been made flesh in Christ, or better still that Jesus *is* the Word of God made flesh.

It means that it is not only in what Jesus has *said* that we have the fullness of God's revelation concerning himself and concerning what we are to become through the actual experience of him offering his own life to us. It means above all that in what Jesus has *done*, and primarily in his Cross, he has achieved and therefore revealed once for all the design of God: that of adopting us to be his sons. This is to be understood not as a figure of speech— implying the greatest possible benevolence towards us, but in stark truth to the effect that what was in Christ on the Cross may be truly in us—his total self-dedication to the Father, the "knowledge" the Father had of him and of us all in him from all eternity. It means finally that in what Jesus *is*, in the ultimate state of his being, as crucified once for all and now and for ever risen from the dead and ascended into heaven whence he is able to send his Spirit into our hearts, he reveals himself as the creative word of this new and definitive creation, according to which word and through which word we are to be born again to a heavenly inheritance.

This is exactly what St Paul in his own way meant when he spoke of the "mystery". The "mystery" especially in the first Epistle to the Corinthians is the whole design of God for man, hidden until then even from the angels, becoming known to all people now in and through the Cross. And that design, as it will be more explicitly expressed in the Epistle to the Colossians, is to reconcile man with God (and simultaneously to reconcile man with himself) in the body of God's only Son offered on the Cross. Therefore the "mystery" is Christ himself, but Christ now seen as the head of a mystical body in which through the power of his Cross we are to be made one by being made together children of God in his only Son. And finally the "mystery" is God himself as he becomes truly and fully known to us through the Cross and in Christ, in so far as in Christ are hidden all the treasures of his wisdom just as in him alone is revealed the fullness of his love. For of that love the final revelation is the Cross, as Paul explains in the fifth chapter of the Romans, when he says that "God has shown his love for us—or better: commended his love to us—in that while we were yet sinners Christ died for us" (5:8; see the whole context).

But the whole mystery—the mystery of the Cross, the mystery of Christ, the mystery of God—is not only communicated *by* the Church, that is to say by its preaching, but is fully revealed *in* the Church, that is to say by what the Church becomes (see *Eph.* 3:10 and the whole context, also 1:22-3), or by what is being done in the Church. For the Church is the body of Christ, which means "the fullness of him who fulfils himself fully in it". Once again in the Church as in Christ preaching the word is one, although in a somewhat different way, with doing and being the word in its fulfilment.

This truth is to be seen first of all in the Eucharist. The Eucharistic celebration can be regarded as the building of the Church by itself. In that it is endowed with the apostolic ministry, the Church announces there the word of Christ, the word of the Cross, the word which is Christ crucified and risen again to become our head. And having been announced in that way by the apostolic preaching of the Gospel, the perfect word of God in Christ finds in the Church its fulfilment, which is that of Christ himself. In the sacramental sacrifice the Church is made one with the body of Christ once dying on the Cross and now risen for ever, so as to reconcile (with the Father and between themselves) all men brought together to a common participation in that selfsame body now given to them as their common food.

Here we come to the centre of our study, to the point where the most intimate connection between word and sacrament can be seen and understood. Three things are to be kept in mind in order to arrive at that. The first is the reality of the word which we have seen as coming to its climax in Christ, but as the fulfilment of a line drawn without a breach from its first utterance to Abraham. The second is the exact meaning of the "apostolate"

on which the Church is built, and which will remain its function
to the end. And the third is the way in which the "apostolate"
of the Church is intended to convey to us the content of the word
of Christ, of the word which in its full actuality is Christ.

Let us then first summarize what has been said of the reality
of God's word. It is the reality of a design of God concerning us
but inseparable from the revelation of the name of God himself,
that is to say his own life, his own being, since that design is to
make of us also sons of the heavenly Father. Therefore, it is when
the only Son is given to us in full reality that the word of God is
both announced and made real for us in its whole actuality. This
happens on the Cross when the love of the heavenly Father in
his Son made man assumes into itself the reality of our sinful and
mortal condition, and by so doing transforms it into the reality
of the risen and ascended Christ.

Now this word of salvation, of reconciliation, of the new
creation in Christ is to be brought to us by the apostolate of the
Church, and more definitely by the apostolate of those who are
made the foundation stones of the Church, namely, the apostles
whom Christ himself has chosen, and all those whom they will
associate with themselves for the perpetuation of their mission.
That is to say, they are to bring to all mankind that same saving
word that is Christ himself, the actuality of his Cross and of what
mankind in him has become through the Cross. How can that
be effected? Only through the mystery of the apostolate, as the
Gospel itself teaches. The apostles, or their successors the bishops,
together with the priests as co-operators of the bishops, are
apostles in the sense that, as he expressed it, he has sent them just
as he had been sent by the Father. It means that he who sends
them will be in them, so that they will not only say *his* word, but
he will be in them saying it with that unique power and reality
it has in him and in him alone. Nothing other than that can
explain his declaration: "Whoever receives you receives me, and
whoever receives me receives the Father who has sent me. Whatever you bind on earth shall be bound in heaven, and whatever
you loose on earth shall be loosed in heaven . . .", and so on.

Now, to understand this exact meaning of the Christian
apostolate, we may recall the Jewish "shaliah" of which the

Greek "apostolos" is a direct translation. The "shaliah" also was "a man who had been sent", but in the precise sense that he who had sent him was supposed to be in him who had been sent, in such a way that anything done by his ambassador was accounted done by the principal himself. The Rabbis said: "The shaliah of a man is like himself", and they gave as an example the story of Elija acting as the shaliah of Abraham and Isaac. When he has chosen Rebecca for the latter, and she has accepted, she is considered not as Isaac's bride-to-be, but as his married wife already, although they have never yet even met. Now, of course, all that was legal fiction. But it is clear from the Gospel that Jesus in choosing and sending his apostles pointed to this fiction intending to constitute it a mysterious but true reality. And this was the significance of such words as "All authority in heaven and on earth has been given to me . . . and lo, I am with you always, to the end of the world" (*Mt.* 28:18-20), and the special gift of this Spirit, as we see it especially in *John* 20:21, is that which will make it fully real: "As the Father has sent me, so I send you. And when he had said this he breathed on them and said to them: Receive the Holy Spirit. If you forgive the sins of anyone, they are forgiven; if you retain the sins of anyone, they are retained".

Therefore, once again, it is not only the word of God with its true meaning which is to be announced by the apostles, but it is the word of God in its active, personal reality as it was found incarnate in Jesus that is to be presented through the apostles, through their apostolate.

But where or how are we to find it in its full and permanent actuality? In the sacrament, and first of all in the Eucharistic celebration. The word of reconciliation, and the atoning word of the Cross, is proclaimed there to the people of God to make it in truth this people by making it the body of his Son in whom all are to be reconciled. Announced in the Gospel, seen as the fulfilment of all the scriptures, it is made actual fact in the sacred meal, in the sacramental sacrifice.

How are we to understand this? It must be noticed that already in Israel the proclamation of the word of God to man in the context of his chosen people led to some signs in which both God pledged himself to accomplish what he had promised and the people pledged themselves to conform to his demands. This provides us with the significance of the whole ceremonial law, and first of all of the sacrifices, as prescribed by God's own law. It is exactly what was meant by that word "memorial" (in Hebrew "zikkaron") by which they were specified. For as the Protestant exegete Jeremias has shown convincingly,[1] this word "memorial" used in the institution of the Eucharist by Jesus himself: "Do this as a memorial of me", is not to be opposed either to the reality of the presence in the Eucharist, or to its sacrificial character, as the classic Protestant exegesis tried to do. Far from it. The Hebrew memorial, firstly, always implies some permanent presence of the sacred event of God's covenant thus renewed and "remembered" and, secondly, it appeared to the Jews as the sacrifice *par excellence*, as the essence of sacrifice. For in it, on the one hand, we pledge ourselves to obedient faith in God's promises and demands and, on the other hand, we plead to him by presenting him with the tokens he himself has left us of his lasting mercy.

In the Christian sacrament, and above all in the sacramental celebration of the Christian sacrifice, or in the Eucharistic meal, all this meaning not only remains true but even assumes a more complete and perfect reality. Since the Word of God made flesh has presented us with the broken bread and the wine in the cup as his body broken for us and as his blood shed for the new covenant he has provided us with a lasting memorial of his sacrificial death. Since he has sent his apostles to his chosen people not only to tell them his word but to bring them in actual truth that word of salvation which he is, when they according to his ordinance take the bread and cup and say over them his own meaningful words they become for us in a mystical but fully real way his very body and blood. Then, just as God was in Christ on the Cross reconciling the world to himself so, too, Christ now comes to us that we may be reconciled in him with God. The reconciliation has been made once for all in the body of Christ on the Cross. But it becomes ours when we are made the mystical body of Christ, his Church, when we partake of this sacrificed body in the Eucharistic meal.

[1] Cf. *The Eucharistic Words of Jesus*, London 1955.

Therefore, the whole content of the word of God which came to its full and lasting perfection in the Son of God made man and crucified is now in the sacrament made our own. What has been enacted once for all, for the salvation of all mankind, here and now becomes *our* salvation. The Church having heard the Gospel word of reconciliation is made in the Eucharist the mystical body of Christ, partaking in his death and resurrection through partaking in his real body once broken now risen from the dead and become the spiritual temple of that Spirit of God who will make our own bodies similar temples.

Let us notice that everything which mediates to us the word in its full reality depends wholly on the word for its realization. For what is it that gives the sacrament its content if not the words of institution, the words by which Christ expressed his will to make them for us efficacious signs of his grace? And what is it that makes of the meal now taking place Christ's own sacramental sacrifice if not the word by which he chose and sent to us his apostles, so that their words should continue and be his, their deeds his deeds? Here we have the most wonderful reality, but nothing magical. All depends on a word of God to man, expressing his sovereign power and almighty love, and addressed to obedient faith, to create love in man out of God's own love.

The consecrating words of the Eucharist are not a kind of trick, like those of a beneficent wizard, by which the priest can operate at will a stupendous wonder. They are in direct continuity with the words of the Gospel, creating in us that faith without which the sacrament would avail nothing for us. By this daily renewed memorial of the words of institution pronounced by those whom the Lord made flesh has commissioned and endowed with the power of the Spirit to bring its truth and reality to his people, the memorial of the Cross itself is re-presented in full truth and reality both as a perfect sacrifice to God and as the sacrament *par excellence* for men.

The Eucharist is the sacrament *par excellence* because it is the ever-renewed sacramental re-presentation of the one sacrifice that has been constituted the source of all sacramental grace, and because in it we can see as it were the transition from the word announced to the word communicated in its full reality.

What has been said of the Eucharist is true also of all the other sacraments.

If the Eucharist is central among them (as we have explained in our other paper), we can say with St Thomas that the most fundamental, from the point of view of the Church and its being, is ordination. The intimate association which this sacrament realizes between those who are to bring the word to all mankind and this same word made flesh can be named the foundation stone of the whole sacramental order.

However, as St Thomas again says, for the individual Christian it is baptism (together with confirmation, with penance restoring its effects if and when necessary) that plays the fundamental role. It is so because baptism is properly the sacrament of faith, as the Fathers call it. It is baptism which opens us to a reception of the word which is to save us by conforming us to and uniting us with itself. As the word united with grace is the principle of our salvation as the gift of God, so faith is the principle of our salvation as our acceptance of that gift. However, that acceptance or rather its possibility is itself a primary gift of grace. Baptism, therefore, is the fundamental sacrament in that it enables us to receive the word of God, not as something foreign to our nature, but as the renewal of our true nature assumed into a super-natural being—this being the proper function of faith. It means, then, that the whole sacramental order, as it is based upon the living communication of the word of God through the apostolate of the Church, is also directed to produce its genuine accept-ance through faith. What faith? That faith which is the response of our thinking and willing personality to the personal disclosure of God's own personality (or rather "heart" as the Bible would say) in his word announced so that the incarnate Word taking to itself our human nature may shape it into the mystical body of Christ.

Here at last we can see how the Protestants were right in describing the sacrament as a *verbum visible* and how they were wrong. They were not wrong in that they went too far in their way, but in that they stopped only half-way. They saw in the word only the word announced, and therefore in the sacrament nothing else than a more material—thus easier to grasp but less satisfactory—transcription of its meaning. Accordingly, the efficacy of the sacrament as that of the word preached was only to create and sustain our faith in a purely psychological way. To faith alone, as through its own power, was committed the task of seizing upon God's gift of grace.

The Catholic doctrine is rather that of itself the word announced, since it is the word of God in Christ still spoken by Christ himself in his ministry, tends to create and to give the reality of grace, at the same time as it evokes faith in our hearts not by a merely psychological effect but by its own innate power. Therefore, faith in the sacrament does not seize grace by its own power, but is rather itself the first gift to be awakened by divine grace as the object and product of the word, of that word which is God made man in Christ and brought to us by the chosen ministers of Christ, in the chosen tokens of his word.

Sacramental Spirituality

SEAN FAGAN

A real weakness in Christian instruction at the present time,
and even in the teaching of theology, is to divide doctrine
and Christian life into separate compartments. On the one
hand there is dogma, revealing to us the truth about God,
and on the other hand the moral code teaching us how to
live; on one side the sacraments, exterior means of salvation,
without our really knowing how or why they work, and on
the other side prayer and the interior life, entirely personal
and incommunicable, by which certain chosen souls are supposed to arrive at a state of perfection outside the ordinary.[1]

THIS criticism of the Dominican theologian, Fr Roguet, is
echoed by many, and though the new trend in moral theology
aims to remedy the defect, it must be admitted that the effects of
the division are very much still with us and pose a problem for
pastoral practice. Good-living Christians do appreciate the sacraments, but many fail to integrate them fully into their spiritual
lives. People will admit that they sometimes wonder just how
essential to one's spiritual life is frequent reception of the sacraments. Not merely the laity, but even priests and religious are

[1] A.-M. Roguet, O.P., *The Sacraments, Signs of Life*, London 1954, 161.

often surprised to discover that their spirituality is not really
sacramental, that the sacraments have only a marginal place in
their scheme of things. One has only to glance at the shelves of
convent libraries to see how few titles mention the sacraments.
and it is possible to read through very many books treating *ex
professo* of the spiritual life without finding more than a passing
reference to the sacraments as a source of grace and sanctity.

The root cause of this weakness in Christian teaching was the
practical need to separate dogmatic and moral theology as
scholastic disciplines. But it is not unlikely that the attitude of
mind to which this dichotomy gave rise was strengthened in many
people by two factors, namely the magical mentality and a gross
misunderstanding of the meaning of the expression *ex opere
operato* applied to the sacraments.

THE MAGICAL MENTALITY

Personal reflection on our own experience and observation of
the mental development of children will show that it is no easy
matter to arrive at a correct theological attitude towards the
sacraments. A recent psychological experiment[2] seems to indicate
that this slowness in acquiring a sacramental mentality is caused
by the difficulty of overcoming the magical mentality which is so
marked a feature of our early years. Strangely enough, it was dis-
covered that there was very little direct relationship between
intelligence and the proper sacramental attitude in the subjects
examined. The governing factor was rather general psychological maturity and proper spiritual training.

Man has a natural inclination to seek security, power and love
by means of certain rites. People make presents or carry out
various activities to attain this security, and the tendency is to
be seen even in infants, when they give orders to inanimate objects
and repeat magic formulas. The magical mentality seems to increase between the ages of six and twelve, when children try to
increase their power over external reality by ritualistic practices.

[2] André Godin, S.J., Soeur Marthe, D.C., "Magic Mentality and Sacramental Life in Children of 8 to 12 years", *Lumen Vitae*, 15 (1960), 277-96.

This primitive tendency is often carried over into their religious life, as shown by their attachment to pious objects or their attitude to prayers, which must be said with scrupulous attention to every word lest the slightest omission result in the petition not being granted. In short, the magical mentality seeks to obtain spiritual advantages by almost exclusively material means. When it extends to the sacramental life of the child it leads to serious confusion. Many young people think that the sacraments are efficacious signs in the sense that once the rite has been physically carried out they automatically produce the spiritual effect. Some fail to realize the importance of contrition in confession and think that the sign of the cross accompanying the absolution is sufficient. They often expect Holy Communion of itself to help them through an examination or give them the gift of purity. These beliefs are common enough among young people, and they linger on in the minds of many who are no longer young. Psychological tests in this field would indicate that development of a correct sacramental mentality increases as the subject gradually frees himself from the magical mentality and this in turn depends on his psychological growth towards maturity.

A MISCONCEPTION

A sacramental spirituality therefore presupposes some achievement in the line of psychological maturity. Defects that have been carried over from infancy in this field are one obstacle to a proper appreciation of the sacraments. Maturity alone, however, is not sufficient. It is simply a necessary prerequisite. What is really needed is a proper spiritual training in the light of sound theological principles. The purely technical expression *ex opere operato* has not always been properly understood. It was chosen by the Council of Trent as denying that the dispositions of the recipient or the merits of the minister are the sole ground of efficacy in sacramental causality[3]. But its frequent use on the

[3] *Denz.* 851. The sacraments as visible signs are a divine guarantee of the presence of God's grace. Scripture constantly emphasizes God's faithfulness to his promises, and the sacraments are among his most solemn promises. However, God's obligation of faithfulness is not to man, but to himself in the person of his Divine Son (cf. Otto Semmelroth, *Vom Sinn der Sakramente*, Frankfurt am Main 1960, 103).

catechetical level misled many into over-emphasis on the activity of God to the neglect of personal preparation. It is quite true that it is God who sanctifies us, that it is not our dispositions which cause the grace imparted, but we must not forget that our faith, devotion and fervour are necessary conditions for our full reception of the grace. Again the phrase *non ponentibus obicem* was used to indicate the dispositions of the recipient, but this too was open to misunderstanding, and its interpretation in terms of passivity helped to confirm the magical understanding of the *ex opere operato* expression. It was easy to forget that, except in the case of infant baptism, the expression "not to place an obstacle" merely indicates the minimum, not the maximum, requirement. As technical terms, these expressions state very clearly a precise aspect of the doctrine they were meant to express. But for a fuller understanding of the doctrine and a deeper appreciation of the sacraments the latter should be seen in a wider context. They are not simply medicinal helps for fallen nature, but the privileged ground for personal encounter with Christ. Properly understood, they are not a devotional extra, a fringe benefit for certain souls, but rather the means *par excellence* given us by God himself for our sanctification and union with him.

CATHOLICISM ESSENTIALLY SACRAMENTAL

The Christian life cannot be understood apart from the central fact of the Incarnation of the Son of God. Christ is our mediator with the Father. He is the way, the truth and the life. In him we "live and move and have our being". Our life as Christians is not mere imitation of him as a model, but life in him, life for him. As he himself has told us, and St Paul has so often repeated, it is personal and intimate union with him, with the Word Incarnate. Now the motive for the Incarnation was not merely that man would thereby be enabled to know and love God more easily under visible form, but rather that the divine person wished to enter into the closest possible union with the whole human race. God came to the race through the vehicle of his humanity, through visible, material nature. He wished his flesh to be a life-giving flesh, a real instrument for the supernatural activity of God on the members of his mystical body. Christ, our founder and our head, is the sacrament of God, and we misunderstand the religion he founded if we fail to see that it is essentially sacramental[4]. As Scheeben puts it: "So great was the blessing which the Incarnation of the God-man shed over matter, that the flesh could become, and was made to become, the vehicle of the Holy Spirit. And the earth, to which man owes his bodily origin and his bodily nourishment, could become, and was made to become, his spiritual mother, while earthly elements were changed into spiritual, supernatural foods for him".[5]

The Incarnation as an existential fact took place at a particular point in human history, but it is true to say that it extends itself in time and space, prolonging itself as Christ comes to birth again in each human soul. Now God's coming to the individual soul, like his first entrance into the human family, is not merely in the purely spiritual contact of faith, but is a real, almost bodily person-to-person encounter through the sacraments of the Church. By the hypostatic union of Christ's humanity with his divinity God's power came down to earth. It is in and through that humanity that it comes to us, and since we no longer have sight of the God-man in our midst it reaches us through those acts of Christ which are the seven sacraments. In the sacraments the historical life and death of Christ, with all their sanctifying power, are freed from their historical limitations and brought in concentrated, dynamic form into the present.

The sacraments therefore are so linked with the very essence of Catholicism that it is impossible to be a Catholic without sharing in them. While we cannot say exactly when one is culpably neglecting to use these privileged means of grace, since neither God nor the Church has commanded their frequent reception, it is not an exaggeration to claim that in the present economy all grace is sacramental because given in virtue of a sacrament received either actually or in desire. Development of this theme would enable us to understand the central position of the sacraments in the spiritual life and overcome the dualism that some writers seem implictly to presuppose in the Christian's

[4] "Non est enim aliud Dei sacramentum nisi Christus". St Augustine, *Ep.* 187, 34; PL 38, 845.
[5] M. J. Scheeben, *The Mysteries of Christianity*, St Louis 1951, 566.

path to sanctity. Spiritual books seem to deal mainly with the subjective activity necessary for sanctification and only occasionally mention sacramental action. The impression is often given that these are two different ways of obtaining the same grace, two separate paths to holiness. Such an impression is entirely false, and it leads to an even greater misconception. Since the subjective activity is something very much in the field of consciousness, where the cause and effect relationship is quickly noted, there sometimes follows a lessening of appreciation with regard to the efficacy of the sacraments. In other words, while the misunderstood expression *ex opere operato* minimizes the place of personal activity, over-emphasis on personal activity leaves little room for Christ's work on the soul through the sacraments.

The balanced view is not simply a compromise. The solution does not mean that each of these two paths contributes its separate share towards the sanctification of the individual. In fact, they are not merely complementary parts, but two closely related, interpenetrating phases of a single, unified process. Sacred Scripture emphasizes both the need for subjective faith and reception of the sacraments for justification and growth in sanctity, though it does not enter into detail about the inter-relation of the two. Theologians have argued about the mechanics of the relationship and discussed the problems of infant baptism and confession with only attrition which obtains the forgiveness normally received through contrition. These difficulties can only be solved in the light of the Christology of grace.[6]

ALL GRACE IS SACRAMENTAL

The grace of Christ imitates its founder. The Word was made flesh, and the share he gives us in his divine life which we call grace not only divinizes us, but also operates dynamically in our most material acts. Just as soul and body operate as one unit, so grace and nature are found together in the spiritual life. Though essentially supernatural, grace becomes incarnate and manifests itself under conditions of time and space. To this extent we may

[6] Cf. Karl Rahner, "Personale und sakramentale Frömmigkeit", *Geist und Leben*, 25 (1952: 6), 412-29. (Eng. tr. in *Theological Investiagtions II.*, London, 1963).

say that it is quasi-sacramental. But grace has likewise a social nature, in so far as the life of the head is intended to flow into each of the members of the mystical body, and in the sacraments, the vital acts of the Church founded by Christ, it becomes not only incarnate but public and almost tangible. To use a metaphor from Karl Rahner, just as even the private and ordinary actions of the citizens of a country reflect the life and culture of that country, so the intimate movements of the soul in the spiritual life will reflect the divine origin of the grace at work. But certain actions like marriages, wills and various civil contracts, require a corresponding official and public act on the part of the governing authority, and in the same way certain steps in the spiritual life call for the intervention of the Church's public and social structure. This is the case of the sacraments, those earthly manifestations in symbolic signs of the personal acts of Christ carried out by the minister of his Church. Grace cannot be received in its fulness except in the Church through the sacraments. Thus by baptism a person is united with Christ not only interiorly by faith but "corporally" as St Thomas says. Thus God's grace is individual and subjective, and at the same time ecclesiastical; interior and spiritual, and yet incarnate; private and nevertheless public. It is the same grace at work. In man's step towards God he is brought into living communication with the mystical body of Christ, and the life of this body flows out to him, not merely after he has become a member, but even reaches out to meet him half-way as it were. In the case of infant baptism, for example, "the faith of the Church contributes to its efficacy", St Thomas tells us[7]. In the case of the sinner who intends to go to confession, the sorrow he has for his sins and the desire to be forgiven enable him to benefit from the sacrament of penance long before he confesses to the priest[8].

[7] *S. theol.*, III, 39, 5.

[8] It is Christ who calls to the sinner interiorly through the promptings of the Holy Spirit and he completes through his minister what he has begun in the sinner's heart. The sacrament thus "brings about" and "completes" the sinner's conversion. Perfect contrition, including as it does the intention to confess, brings sanctifying grace and this grace is already sacramental in the sense that it is the first step in the sacrament just as absolution is the final one. But it is not complete. The full sacramental grace can be had only through the intervention of the Church in the administration of the sacrament. Cf. Paul Anciaux, "La dimension ecclésiale de la pénitence chrétienne", *Collectanea Mechliniensia*, NS 31 (1961), 465-82.

Grace, therefore, reaches its culmination of physical reality and intensity in the sacraments. In every sacrament the believer enters more deeply into the living bond which the community of the Church has with the sanctifying mysteries of its head. But the encounter with Christ is full and personal only when the recipient is open and sensitive to the advances of the divine power. It must be remembered that the sacraments have no automatic effect, no therapeutic value. Religious teachers sometimes wonder why their students later find their way to prison or lose their faith when they had been made go to the sacraments each week during their school years. Increased frequency in receiving the sacraments does not automatically benefit one's spiritual life. A common stumbling-block, in fact, is the daily communicant whose only example is mediocrity, whose practical Christianity is far below the level of many who rarely approach the sacraments. Grace has not been lacking in these cases, but the channels through which the divine life flows to the recipient were not kept open by the latter. It is true that subjective dispositions are not the *cause* of grace, but at the same time they are more than a mere occasion. They do not contribute to the *validity* of the sacrament, since the divine initiative takes precedence over our human striving, but they are a true measure of sacramental grace. Indeed the general opinion of theologians is that differences in grace received from the sacraments are to be attributed solely to the differences of disposition in the recipients. The only limitation on sacramental grace is the capacity of the receiving subject.

Hence the need for sacramental spirituality. Fruitful reception of the sacraments presupposes a properly disposed soul, a spiritual life actively directed towards God. But it would be a mistake to think of the work of disposing oneself as something distinct from the sacraments. The sacraments themselves are the most potent means towards the acquisition of proper dispositions. When the sacraments are seen not as coins for a slot-machine which will dispense grace, but as the prolongation of Christ's sacred humanity, the divinely-appointed means of personal encounter with the glorified Lord, they will enkindle those sentiments of faith, hope and love which open the soul to fuller participation in divine life.

SACRAMENTS OF FAITH, HOPE AND CHARITY

The sacraments are first and foremost sacraments of the faith. Speaking of the influence of the historical mysteries of Our Lord's life, St Thomas says: "Though corporeal, Christ's passion because united to the divinity possesses a spiritual power also. Therefore it acquires its efficacy through spiritual contact, that is through faith and the *sacraments of faith*".[9] Each sacrament invokes faith, is defined and measured by faith. Again, St Thomas tells us: "We are saved through faith in Christ . . . Moreover, we have sacraments, *signs protesting that faith* by which a man is justified"[10] As protestations of faith, the sacraments are not mere verbal expressions of an internal act of faith, but positive acts of witnessing, gestures, rites, signs-in-action. The witnessing they imply calls for a personal involvement, an undertaking which commits the whole personality. The sacraments properly received with full awareness of their import are the most outstanding acts of faith of which we are capable. Belief in the articles of the Creed is an act of faith, but reception of the sacraments focusses our faith to a burning intensity and extends it to the entire mystery of our Redemption. This is because each sacrament in its own way sums up the whole supernatural economy of God's dealing with his children. They all make present the mysteries of Christ's passion and death, they sanctify us with sanctifying grace, the infused virtues and gifts, and they are essentially directed towards our final happiness. In a word, the object of the act and virtue of faith and the object signified by the sacraments are one and the same. Considered theologically, therefore, even apart from the grace they confer, reception of the sacraments far surpasses any private profession of faith. But they also excel from the psychological point of view. In the act of faith we assent to a truth. The fulness of faith demands a personal commitment, a total involvement. But, because of the soul's natural dependence on the body, when we see it acted out visibly in the symbolic rites of the sacraments we become wholeheartedly involved. The risen Lord has ascended to heaven and is now seen only in the dark-

[9] *S. theol.*, III, 48, 6 ad 2.
[10] *S. theol.*, III, 61, 4.

ness of faith. But that faith throbs to life with a new fervour and a
special intensity when his mysterious presence and sanctifying
power come to us in the familiar things of earth—the cleansing
water of baptism, the spiritual food of the Eucharist, the firm
pressure of the ordaining hand. Frequent contact with these saving symbols in the full awareness of their symbolism naturally
leads to a life of faith.

But faith has its proper role at the very heart of sacramental
efficacy. It is a welcoming, a receiving. It is the subject's faith that
receives the instrumental activity of the sign which God uses to
produce grace. Instrumental activity requires contact, hence the
sacraments must have real contact with the soul that they sanctify.
Now the material element in the various sacraments reaches
only the body and the sense faculties. But the material elements
(rites and words) are grasped by the intelligence of the baptized
as a sign of the invisible reality which the sacraments produce in
the soul. Since this invisible reality is not only spiritual but supernatural, the intelligence must be enriched by the divine gift of
faith. Contact is made in the mind through the supernatural power
of faith. To the eyes of the unbaptized, water is simply water, the
sacred species merely bread and wine. To the eyes of faith, however, the ablution of baptism is at the same time death to sin with
Christ and resurrection to a new life, while the Eucharist is the
body of the risen Lord himself. For the believer, the forgiveness
of sin is as real as the visible healing of the sick. Faith assures the
necessary contact between the sacramental, efficacious sign and
the soul it sanctifies[11].

Thus, not only does the objective faith of the Church enter into
the very nature of the sacraments as protestations of faith, but the
faith of the recipient or at least the collective faith of the believing
faithful integrally participates in the sacramental order as a kind
of faculty for receiving grace. Just as the natural faculties improve

[11] In the case of infant baptism and valid, but unfruitful reception of certain
sacraments, the faith in question is the faith of the Church. "The faith of the
whole Church profits the infant through the operation of the Holy Spirit who
unites the Church and communicates the goods of one to another" (*S. theol.*,
III, 68, 9 ad 2). Valid reception requires the intention to do or receive what
the Church intends in the sacramental rites, but such an intention, even
without personal faith, implies reference to the faith of the Church and
enables the recipient to receive at least the sacramental character or corresponding mark, though not the grace of the sacrament.

with use, the supernatural power of faith is increased by exercise, and increase in faith means greater capacity for the reception of grace. Sacramental activity and subjective dispositions therefore are correlative, interdependent aspects of the one sanctifying process.

Grounded in faith, the Christian life is buoyed up by hope. St Peter in his first epistle tells us that "We are to share an inheritance that is incorruptible, inviolable, unfading; it is stored up for you in heaven"[12]. Hope is one of the most characteristic elements of Christianity, the centre of gravity of the spiritual life. The Christtian is essentially a person who hopes. But this does not mean that he is one who is merely waiting for something in the future. Just as faith gives us real and present contact with the risen Lord, so the object of hope is both present and future at the same time. We hope, not for what we do not have, but rather for what we do not have in all its fulness. Now the sacraments properly received strengthen this hope. While preparing us for the fulfilment of our union with God, and indeed giving us a foretaste of it in the grace they confer, they essentially point to the beyond. The encounter we have with Christ in the sacraments intensifies our confidence in the promises of God and leaves us in a state of spiritual tension between the joy of a real possession already begun and the expectation of fulness to come.

Natural hope is purely individual. Man instinctively seeks his own good, his own happiness. Were supernatural hope the same, he would consider his own personal salvation and happiness the sole object of his hope. But faith makes us children of the Church, members of the mystical body, sharing its life and hope, so that hope is really itself only if it is nourished on charity. The Christian cannot be indifferent to the fate of his neighbour. His very calling as a follower of Christ commits him to personal involvement in the sanctification of his fellows. His love of God is unreal unless it includes all God's children. The authentic Christian therefore is not one who is pre-occupied with self-perfection, but one who is deeply conscious of his social nature. Here again the sacraments are the ideal means to sharpen this consciousness and cement the bonds that link us to one another. None of the sacra-

[12] 1 *Pet.* 1 :4.

ments has a purely private character. All are essentially social. They are sacraments of the Church, instruments of unity[13]. Baptism is not merely an individual cleansing, but a new birth into a spiritual family. Even penance, which seems such a personal affair, is essentially ecclesial. The sinner confesses to the priest because he believes he encounters Christ through the Church, just as it has been the Church that has suffered harm through his sins. He confesses and accepts his penance in order to re-establish communion, to take his place once more in the community and participate more fully in the life of grace. But full participation in the Church's life involves participation in her mission, and her mission is to all nations. Sacramental spirituality therefore keeps one alive to the call of the apostolate, and gives the necessary helps to carry it out effectively.

The spiritual life is a life of faith, hope and charity. It will be readily seen that the sacraments are not an alternative to the theological virtues, a separate path to holiness, but rather the privileged channels through which we are given these divine gifts. The theological virtues have God as their object, and it is the same God in the person of his incarnate Son whom we meet in the sacraments. There can be no dualism therefore in the spiritual life. Christian spirituality cannot be other than sacramental, and if it is not so there is something wrong.

The above remarks on sacramental spirituality have put considerable and understandable emphasis on the psychological aspect. The more the sacraments are understood and appreciated the more the soul opens itself to receive their benefits. There is endless matter for meditation in the sacred symbolism of the sacramental system, and since the realities signified are the supernatural mysteries of Christ's passion and death and indeed the whole economy of salvation we can never fully exhaust their possibilities as food for contemplation. But it would be a serious error to imagine that the sacraments only produce their effects by arousing pious thoughts and feelings in the mind and heart of the

[13] "Since the sacraments are the means of salvation they should be understood as instruments of unity. As they make real, renew or strengthen man's union with Christ, by that very fact they make real, renew or strengthen his union with the Christian community" (H. de Lubac, S.J., *Catholicism*, London 1962, 32).

recipients. The sacraments are not merely sacred signs but efficacious signs which produce the supernatural realities they signify. They not only give an increase in faith as a result of their character of sign, but they bring a real share in the divine life with all the supernatural powers that go with it. The faith and charity of the recipient are the measure of the grace received, the necessary condition for its reception, but the sacraments are not merely for the stimulation of faith. They are effective not simply in producing psychological changes in the believer but in producing something which only divine power can produce.

We have already said that the sacraments bring us into personal contact with Christ. The experience is one of encounter, of dialogue. When Moses came down from the mountain after his converse with God his face shone with a strange radiance. But our contact with the Lord produces a much deeper effect. It brings about a change in the soul itself. In baptism we are conformed to Christ. As Christ died to mortal life, we die to sin, redeemed by his sufferings. As he rose to a glorified state of life, we are brought to a new life of holiness. Our rebirth and transformation by grace unites us with the risen Christ, so that there is conformity between the Eternal Son of God and the adopted sons who henceforth become his brothers. We are given a real share in the divine life itself. We are changed, not merely psychologically, but ontologically and supernaturally. A greater awareness of what the sacraments actually do for us would produce a more sacramental spirituality.

SACRAMENTAL GRACES

In his *Mysteries of Christianity*[14] Scheeben distinguishes between what he calls the "medicinal sacraments" (penance and extreme unction) and "sacraments of consecration", because the latter dedicate us to a supernatural destiny and assign us to a special permanent place in the mystical body of Christ. The distinction is indeed valid, but at the same time it is true to say that both healing and consecration are to be found in all of the sacra-

[14] Pp. 572-9.

ments. Though the medicinal sacraments forge no new organic bond with Christ, they do consecrate us to a renewal of supernatural life, and on the other hand, while the Eucharist, for example, unites us intimately with our divine Lord, it is also a remedy of strength for our weakness. All of the sacraments, therefore, repair the harm done to our nature by sin, and they do this precisely in so far as they make us partakers in the divine nature. This share in the divine nature is what theologians describe as sanctifying grace. It is difficult to speak of this mysterious reality except by analogies which can never convey the full meaning of that intimate personal union with God which changes our whole being. Sacred Scripture speaks of our sins being blotted out[15], of the new life given to us[16], of our being sons of God[17], sharers in the divine nature[18]. All the sacraments, when properly received, either give us this grace or increase it when we already have it. It is true that God's grace is not limited to the seven sacraments, that there are other means of receiving or increasing sanctifying grace. But the sacraments are the divinely-appointed channels surpassing all others. In fact, grace given outside the sacraments is never without at least implicit reference to the sacraments. This is especially true for the practising Catholic, thanks to a further effect of the sacraments which theologians call sacramental grace. This is a lasting effect of the sacraments reaching far beyond the time of their reception. Were the sacraments to confer only sanctifying grace there would be no need for a variety of sacraments. Each of the seven sacraments has its own sacramental grace.

Theologians are not agreed on the precise nature of this special grace. Some, following Cajetan, hold that it is simply sanctifying grace together with a right or a title to actual graces when they are needed to fulfil the purpose of the sacrament. Others, with various modifications, follow St Thomas and maintain that it is an infused habit distinct from sanctifying grace though flowing from it like all the infused virtues. According to this view it is something like an infused virtue or gift of the Holy Ghost. In the

[15] *Acts* 3:19.
[16] *John* 6:57; 10:28-9; *Gal.* 2:20.
[17] *John* 1:12; *Gal.* 4:6-7; *Rom.* 8:17.
[18] 1 *Pet.* 1:4.

natural order the powers of growth, movement and thought are distinguished from the principle of life which is their source. In the same way the various sacramental graces are distinct from sanctifying grace from which they flow. What Pius XI said of the effects of matrimony may be applied to each of the seven sacraments.

> For this sacrament, if its fruit is not frustrated by the obstacle of conscious mortal sin, not only increases in the soul the permanent principle of supernatural life, which is sanctifying grace, but also adds special gifts, good impulses, and seeds of grace, amplifying and perfecting the powers of nature, and enabling the recipients not only to understand with their minds, but also to relish intimately, grasp firmly, will effectively, and fulfil in deed all that belongs to the state of wedlock and its purposes and duties; it also gives them the right to obtain the help of actual grace whenever they need it for the discharge of their matrimonial tasks.
>
> Christian husbands and wives will find great assistance in frequent meditation upon their state and in an effective remembrance of the sacrament they have received. Let them be constantly mindful that they have been consecrated and strengthened for the duties and dignities of their state by a sacrament whose efficacy, though it does not confer a character, remains nonetheless in perpetuity[19].

In other words, at the reception of each sacrament there is infused into our souls a new power, which can be developed by exercise like the natural powers, or allowed to atrophy for the lack of use. It can never atrophy in the strict sense, since it is not lost except through the loss of sanctifying grace itself, but it can lie dormant and not fully efficacious if we fail to use it. What St Paul wrote to Timothy concerning the sacrament of orders we may take as addressed to ourselves with regard to the sacraments we have received: "I would remind thee to fan the flame of that special grace which God enkindled in thee, when my hands were laid upon thee. The spirit he has bestowed on us is not one that shrinks from danger; it is a spirit of action, of love, and of dis-

[19] *Christian Marriage*, CTS, London 1930, 39-40.

cipline"[20]. These special graces are new powers, dynamic forces
habitually at our disposal to enable us to live a fuller Christian
life. We renounce Satan in baptism, but the renunciation needs
to be repeated many times in the course of a lifetime, and the
sacramental grace of baptism is at work each time we overcome
temptation. It also tends to perfect itself by a longing for the
other sacraments. It is the sacramental grace of confirmation
which enables us to overcome cowardice and human respect as
we make the sign of the cross before and after a meal in a rest-
aurant. Each time we renew our sorrow for sin and unite ourselves more closely to our divine Lord, it is the work of the
graces received at our last confession and Holy Communion.
Penance not only blots out sin but gives us a hunger for the
Eucharist, and Communion not only helps us to avoid sin but
perfects the spiritual life and spurs us to ever closer union. The
sacramental grace of extreme unction enables us to bear suffering
in a supernatural manner. It does not eliminate pain, but illuminates it, giving us a glimpse of its value in the divine plan. The
priest is tempted like the ordinary Christian. When he feels like
neglecting his ministry it is the special grace of order which enables him to overcome the difficulty. The dispositions of the
minister do not affect the efficacy of the sacrament he administers,
but his special grace makes the act fruitful for himself no matter
what its effect on the recipient. Finally, the grace of matrimony
is something which reaches out over the years of married life
and sanctifies even the most insignificant actions of the married
couple. When they show affection for each other or make sacrifices
for their children, they are helped by the special grace of the
sacrament which makes their union like that of Christ with his
Church.

   These special helps given by the sacraments cover every
detail of our human existence. They are so varied that they cannot
be given any special name beyond the generic term of sacramental
graces. St Thomas says of them:

> From the grace which is in the essence of the soul, there
> flows something to repair the defects which arise from sin,

[20] 2 *Tim.* 1:6-7.

and this is diversified according to the diversity of the defects. But, because these defects are not so well known to us as are the the activities made more perfect by the virtues, hence this effect of repairing defects has no special name, as has a virtue, but retains the name of its cause, and is called sacramental grace, to which the sacraments are directly ordered; but this grace cannot exist without the grace which is in the essence of the soul, just as neither can the virtues[21].

Each of the virtues has a specific object, a definite field of action, but the sacramental graces cover too wide an area and reach into too many details to be grouped under special headings. There are so many actions that cannot be labelled under a particular virtue, so many vague weaknesses that have no special name, and these are all catered for by the special graces of each sacrament. We may have sanctifying grace, with its accompanying infused virtues and gifts, apart from direct reception of the sacraments, but in that case we do not receive these special gifts. If the sacraments are sometimes not appreciated as they should be, perhaps it is because we fail to recall, if we have ever fully understood, their far-reaching effects.

Even when received without the proper dispositions, the sacraments are not entirely without effect. Baptism, confirmation and orders confer an indelible character distinct from grace even on a subject who is not properly disposed. It is precisely by means of the sacramental character, and not by means of grace as such, that we are incorporated into the mystical body and are given a share in the priesthood of Christ. A non-baptized person does not receive our divine Lord when he communicates, nor can he consecrate bread and wine by saying "This is my body, this is my blood", even though he intends to do what Christ did. On the other hand, the priest in sin or even in heresy can validly absolve and consecrate. The character imprinted by these three sacraments is of such a nature that they are not repeated. By analogy, however, theologians hold that, apart from the Eucharist[22], the

---

[21] *Comm. Sent.*, In IV D. 1, 1, 4-5, quoted in B. Leeming, S.J., *Principles of Sacramental Theology*, London 1956, 109-10.
[22] Some would hold for no exceptions. Cf. Taymans D'Eypernon, *The Blessed Trinity and the Sacraments*, Dublin 1961, 18.

other sacraments imprint a mark on the soul which is not the indelible character, nor sanctifying grace, but an embellishment of the soul, an exigence of grace, a kind of seed of divine life which fructifies once the obstacle is removed. In this way it can be said that the soul is always enriched by reception of a sacrament, at least in so far as this special mark disposes the soul to receive grace when the obstacle is removed. A Christian couple who marry in the state of mortal sin are guilty of sacrilege, but when they confess their sin the graces of matrimony are said to "revive", without the necessity of repeating the sacrament. This special mark, the *ornatus animae*, consists in a certain resemblance to Christ produced in the soul in varying degrees by the different sacraments. God sees this likeness and loves such a son with the same love with which he loves his Only-begotten. Even in the case of those who put an obstacle in the way of grace, though they lack divine life something of this likeness to Christ remains as a claim on God's goodness. The still-born baby is a grief to its parents, but the parents are not indifferent to the resemblence it bears to the family. The seed of grace implanted by a valid sacrament will come to life when the soil has been properly disposed and the obstacle removed. This does not mean that even sacrilegious reception of the sacraments is better than no sacrament, but these special effects of the sacrament even fruitlessly received enable us to appreciate the privileged position of the sacraments in the spiritual life.

SANCTIFICATION A UNIFIED PROCESS

A thorough understanding of the intimate nature and far-reaching effects of the sacraments would bring us to a more sacramental spirituality. It is not simply a question of deciding on more frequent reception of the sacraments, of giving them a little more thought during our periods of formal mental prayer, but rather of giving our whole spiritual life a sacramental orientation. It is not simply a matter of emphasizing more the sacramental path to God, while not neglecting the ascetical, but of integrating the two into one road to holiness. Some souls even among those who rightly think of the spiritual life in terms of the indwelling of the blessed Trinity fail to make full use of the sacraments because they are hypnotized by the word "grace". They think of the sacraments as producing grace, but fail to make the connection between this and personal intimacy with the three divine persons. The tendency then is to distinguish between ritual, namely the sacraments, and the spiritual life as such, identified with mental prayer and the practice of the virtues. Even in the case of those for whom the word "grace" is not a mental block preventing deeper understanding of the sacraments as personal encounters with Christ, the link with the Trinity is not fully grasped. It is sometimes forgotten that Father, Son and Holy Ghost are really one God, distinct persons but inseparable. In meeting Christ we come into contact with the triune God.

All of the sacraments bring us the acts of Christ, enable us to benefit from the power that goes forth from Christ, but the Eucharist, the most frequently received of all, gives us the fulness of Christ, gives us Christ himself. Unfortunately, it is in this sacrament most of all that our relation with the Trinity is forgotten. Holy Communion brings about perfect union between the human person and the person of the Word who becomes our spiritual food. Natural food is changed into our human substance, but the effect of the Eucharist is to change our souls. Christ gives himself to us, but he transforms us by grace into his own life. St Leo the Great says that "participation in the body and blood of Christ changes us into that which we eat"[23]. Now our mingling with the Word brings us into the closest union with the other two persons. Our divine Lord takes us into the very bosom of the Trinity, making us children of the Father in a new way and embracing us in that personification of love between Father and Son which we call the Holy Spirit. Thus the Eucharist, which at first sight seems to focus attention exclusively on the person of Jesus, really brings us a supreme degree of union with all three divine persons. The same relationship to the Trinity is to be found in all the sacraments. St Paul wrote to the Galatians: "When the appointed time had come God sent out his Son on a mission to

[23] *Sermones*, LXIII, PL 54, 358. "Jesus Christ bears us in himself; we are, if I may dare to say so, more truly his body than his own body is" (Bossuet, *Sermon sur la nécessité des souffrances*, for Palm Sunday).

us . . . to ransom those who were subject to the law, and make us
sons by adoption. To prove that you are sons, God has sent out
the Spirit of his Son into your hearts, crying out in us, Abba,
Father"[24]. Our reception of the sacraments enables us to call
God "Father" with a quality and a depth of meaning impossible
otherwise. To think of the sacraments without positive reference
to the sanctifying work of the Holy Ghost and the indwelling of
the blessed Trinity is a lack of theological insight which distorts
one's view of the spiritual life.

To counter the impression created by the meagre references to
the sacraments in spiritual books one should recall the lives of
the saints. There were some whose circumstances did not allow
frequent reception of the sacraments, but the vast majority
literally lived on them. The saintly Dom Marmion told one of
his correspondents: "I have now divided my day into two parts:
1. I live on my morning Communion; 2. I prepare for the next.
Jesus loves us to profit by our Communion"[25]. To another he
wrote: "Each Communion takes us further and further into the
infinite abyss of the Divinity"[26]. There were many who, like St
Francis Borgia, went to confession every day.

However, it would be a mistake to think that mere frequenting
of the sacraments brings one closer to God. All that the sacramental rites produce infallibly is the *res et sacramentum*, namely
the character in three of the sacraments and a corresponding
mark in the case of the others. For the sacrament to bear its full
fruit there must be active co-operation on the part of the recipient.
This co-operation will be forthcoming to the extent that we know
and appreciate the depth of meaning and the riches of grace to
be found in the sacraments. The mediocrity of some daily com-
municants should not blind us to the value of the sacraments any
more than the abuse of God's gifts of food and drink should
prevent us from appreciating divine goodness. Our spirituality
will be sacramental in so far as we realise that the sacraments are
the essential source of sanctity, that "sacramental grace alone is

[24] *Gal.* 4:4-6.
[25] *The English Letters of Abbot Marmion*, Dublin 1962, 212.
[26] Ibid., 214.

fully Christian, making us like Christ"[27]. The more we are aware of the variety of powers at our disposal in the supernatural organism given to us by the sacraments, the more we can use them. The infused virtues and the gifts of the Holy Ghost are explained as part of moral theology, but too often they are discussed without reference to their source, namely sanctifying grace, and without sufficient emphasis on the manner in which they are effected by the sacraments. How seldom is sacramental grace in the strict sense treated fully in the manuals. On the catechetical level particularly it should be integrated into the normal presentation of the Christian life[28]. The sacraments should be seen not as one among many means to holiness, but as the essential path to God for every Christian. God came to man in the Incarnation, and it is essentially through the sacraments that he wills to reach the individual soul. The sacraments are a kind of further incarnation, a personal involvement on the part of Christ and his Church and on the part of the recipient who is properly disposed. They are a mutual encounter, a personal dialogue between the Word and the soul he comes to possess. In the spiritual order, to live is Christ, and Christ is to be found first and foremost—with a tranquil, moral certainty of the authenticity of his presence—in the sacraments of his Church.

[27] C. Journet, *The Meaning of Grace*, London 1962, 110.
[28] An excellent presentation is E. H. Schillebeeckx, O.P., *Christ, the Sacrament of the Encounter with God*, London 1963, the main themes of which are to be found condensed in the same author's article "The Sacraments: an Encounter with God", in *Christianity Divided*, London 1962, 245-75. Another work which integrates the sacraments into the whole Christian life is B. Häring, C.SS.R., *Gabe und Auftrag der Sakramente*, Salzburg 1962.

The Priest as Minister
of the Sacraments

JOSEPH CUNNANE

The first title of the Roman Ritual, which draws its inspiration from the disciplinary forms of the Council of Trent, succeeds in giving in a very short space quite a remarkable amount of information about the priest's role in the celebration of the sacraments.

It is not easy to condense any further that summary, but we may say that the following are its principal points. First, with regard to the priest's own life: Since the sacraments are the holiest, most useful, and most excellent means for the sanctification and salvation of the faithful instituted by Christ and committed to his Church, the priest must appreciate them. He must be always ready to administer them, and must try by the integrity, chastity and piety of his life to be worthy of his function as their minister. When called upon to administer a sacrament he ought to answer the summons without delay; but taking time, if he has the opportunity, for a little prayer and meditation on the sacred action he is about to perform and some thought and study on the ceremonies involved. On his way to administer the sacrament the priest should be intent on the sacred task he is undertaking and should avoid speaking to anybody on other matters. Both he and his assistants should be properly vested, and he should have and keep clean and in good order all the equipment necessary for celebrating the sacraments.

In the actual celebration of the sacrament the priest must have the intention of doing what the Church does, and ought to strive to have actual or at least virtual attention. He should pronounce every word of the form of the sacrament attentively, distinctly, piously and in a clear voice. The other prayers of the Ritual ought to be recited devoutly and religiously too and generally not from memory but from the Ritual. All the ceremonies and rites ought to be carried out in such a becoming and respectful manner as to command the attention of bystanders and lift up their minds to the thought of heavenly things

Secondly, with regard to the people: It is the duty of the priest to make known to the people, and to repeat often for their benefit that he is always available for the administration of the sacraments when they require him—*quacumque diei ac noctis hora*; and to urge them that they should send for him at once when he is needed without consideration of any inconvenience that may be caused him. In administering the sacraments the priest should, if he can conveniently do so, explain carefully to the people the efficacy and usefulness of the sacraments and the meaning of the ceremonies. At other times too the faithful should be warned about the reverence expected of them whenever they assist at the celebration of the sacraments or receive them. As already mentioned, the actual performance of the sacramental rites ought to be a source of edification to the people.

The programme here outlined for the priest then is a faithful dedication to his duty to administer the sacraments to his people and a continuous effort to appreciate the sacraments himself and to lead his people, by his instructions and by the example of his own reverence for the sacraments, to a fuller appreciation of them. It may be said that such a programme does no more than reflect the average priest's attitude towards his ministry. Whatever other activities he may be called upon to engage in for the religious, cultural, social or economic betterment of his people, the priest is convinced that the fundamental reason and justification for his presence in his parish is the divine mediation of which he is the

instrument. This is his life, it is the basis of his understanding
with his people, the terms of his dedication to their service. He is
with his flock not merely in obedience to the prescriptions of
canon law, but because he knows that this is his task in the
economy of salvation, this is his particular corner of the Lord's
vineyard. And the sacraments, he knows well, with the word of
God, are the principal means put in his hands by Christ and his
Church for the task entrusted to him.

Such a man, whom I have ventured to describe as the average
priest, may well ask: What have the theologians to offer, that
can be of any help to me in my sacramental ministry to my
people? It is obvious that the question can be asked with a certain
amount of impatience, or even cynicism. The priest engaged on the
pastoral mission can regard the theologian in much the same
light as the more old-fashioned farmer regarded the agricultural
instructor: the man of theory who should stick to his book-
learning and not presume to tell hard-working men their business!

We will find that theologians these days have a somewhat
different approach to the sacraments from that of their predecessors. There is of course no question of abandoning traditional teaching, but there is a shifting of emphasis. The theology
of the past might be said to have fostered a rather impersonal
view of a sacrament. It was concerned primarily with the causality of the sacraments. Therefore it thought of the sacrament as
an instrument, a thing to be given by a priest to a more or less
passively-receiving subject on whom this sacred thing caused
grace to be conferred *ex opere operato* provided he placed no
obstacle in its way. Theologians of course always emphasized
the necessity of the good dispositions of the subject for the fruit-
fulness of the sacrament. Nowadays, as a result of a more pastoral
outlook in theology generally, and a deepening of understanding
of the Church's life and liturgy, theologians tend to think of a
sacrament as an *action*, an act of Christ and of his Church, a
symbolic act bringing about an encounter between God and the
Christian, demanding a movement of faith and desire on the
part of the receiving subject. Perhaps we might best summarize
this new outlook by quoting the five short doctrinal principles
prefixed to the *Directoire pour la pastorale des sacrements* issued

by the French Hierarchy to their clergy in April 1951.

1. The sacraments are *acts* of Christ, exercising his priesthood through the ministry of his Church for the glory of God and the salvation of men.

2. The sacraments are also sacred *signs* instituted by Christ, and by the will of Christ himself each of them has its own characteristics and particular notes.

3. The sacraments are *signs of grace*. Efficacious signs, they communicate divine life to man, putting it within his reach according to his various needs and manifesting it to him by the sacramental words, objects and rites.

4. At the same time, they express and realise incorporation into the Church. *Signs of the Church*, the sacraments are also given in the community and with a view to the community, which they are destined to build up and bind together.

5. The sacraments are *signs of faith*; for the recipients of the sacrament, this reception supposes and affirms his faith in Christ and in the Church.

Leaving the further development and explanation of these principles to the theologians, we may ask what value such new approach to the sacraments can have for the priest engaged in their administration, either in that deepening of his own appreciation of the sacraments or in the instruction and edification of his flock which the Roman Ritual has told us to be the duty of the priest.

Being acts of Christ and his Church the sacraments will demand for their celebration an interior and exterior conformity between the sentiments and acts of the minister and those of Christ and his Church. We are already familiar from long use with the phrase "the intention of doing what the Church does". But this expression is generally used in the minimal sense to indicate the bare essentials for the validity of a sacrament. And of course it must not be forgotten that Christ has made the efficacy of the sacraments independent of the personal sanctity of their minister. But once this important truth is safeguarded we can see that the "intention of the Church" must be thought of in a much broader and much more positive sense than this. It must be emphatically stated that it is not in accordance with the intention of the Church

that merely valid sacraments should be celebrated. To suggest otherwise is to take an altogether unworthy view of the
Church as Christ's Sacrament, Christ's Bride, Christ on earth.
If the sacrament were to be regarded merely as an inanimate
"thing" then the Church might conceivably be regarded as being
satisfied provided the thing worked. The priest called on to
administer such a sacrament might also conceivably reach for his
oilstocks in much the same way as a doctor would for his hypo-
dermic syringe, confident that the thing administered would have
the desired effect, if the patient had a sufficiently strong constitution.

But the intention of the Church in administering every sacrament must be seen against the broad background of the story of
God's efforts to draw man to him,—to share his divine life with
man in grace, and to bring man's heart to him in worship. This
story reaches its climax in the redemptive act of Jesus Christ on
Calvary and his prolongation of that act through space and time
in his mystical body, the Church. This redemptive act is now to
be sacramentalized through the faith of Christ's Church for the
benefit of the particular soul about to receive the sacrament. It
is then obviously the intention of Christ and his Church that the
minister, whose official act is to bring about this encounter between the saving Christ and the soul, should himself share to the
greatest possible extent in Christ's and the Church's desire for
the worship of God and the sanctification of man which the
sacrament expresses.

In other words, the priest's own personal sanctity and his
apostolic zeal for the sanctification of his flock ought to make
of his official prayer and act of worship a real personal prayer
for the person receiving the sacrament. As Fr Schillebeeckx
points out . . .

> It is because he is the minister of the Church that this act
> demands essentially of him a personal religious and apostolic
> integration in the sacramental prayer of Christ and his
> Church. The ecclesial administration of a sacrament is there-
> fore normally a personal act manifesting itself in this very
> administration of faith, of apostolic hope and of paternal

redemptive charity, as intercession for the one who receives the sacrament. The minister ought to act not merely as minister of the *visible* Church, but as minister of the *mystery* of the Church.

And he adds further on in the same context:

The normal situation required strictly by the fulness of the Church's being is that of a sacramental ministration in which the minister performs the acts of his office in such a way that they are at the same time an expression of his own personal dedication to the apostolate, and of his will to sanctify the persons to whom he administers the sacraments[1].

It cannot really be said that such a view of the sacramental ministry suggests obligation on us not already implied in our priestly ordination and repeated for our guidance in the Ritual and in the Code of Canon Law. But it does open up a vista of what might be termed pastoral prayer for those of us who are charged with the care of souls. No doubt we all pray for our people. They have a place in our *Memento* at Mass. They are continually asking our prayers, as well as asking us to offer Mass for their intentions. But what of the prayers we offer for them in the administration of the sacraments? To take the two commonest examples, what of the prayers of absolution and the giving of Holy Communion? Repeating these hundreds of times every week, do we make them real personal prayers for each of the people concerned? Are we really conscious of any obligation to do so? And yet these are the prayers that ask the really worth-while things for our people—not just cures for their rheumatics or their sick babies, important as these are in their own way, but the fundamental things, forgiveness of their sins, life ever-lasting, the things that we have been ordained and sent to bring them.

You can of course say that these prayers are offered in the name of Christ and his Church and that this gives them an efficacy independent of us. But it would be wrong to conclude that we have no further duty than merely to say them. The fruit-fulness of these prayers (prescinding again from the *validity* of

[1] E. H Schillebeeckx, *Christ the Sacrament*, London 1963, 124.

the essential form of the sacrament) will depend on the dispositions of the particular people concerned. It may well happen of course, and does, that the person we are absolving or giving Communion to is holier and more advanced in the life of grace than we are. But this, we know, is not by any means always so and is not the normal case contemplated by the Church. We *are* the Church in this particular case, we are the representatives of Christ, and we have the obligation and privilege of carrying out their wishes for this particular soul, not only by our admonitions and by our placing of the matter and form of the sacrament but by our personal prayer and appeal for grace, reflecting all the solicitude of Christ and the Church for God's glory and the salvation of souls.

It is not suggested that the average priest could keep up actual attention to all the prayers of an evening's absolutions or could give rail after rail of Communions without any distractions! Like every other prayer he can only keep struggling with them, doing his best. His success will reflect the general standard of his life of prayer and will inevitably of course affect that standard. But what would be wrong, and would come very near to reducing the sacraments to the level of magic, would be to accept the position of a mere official of the Church in distributing absolutions or Communions, with the vaguely pious intention of doing God's work for souls, no doubt, but without any consciousness of the possiblilties of the apostolate of prayer and spiritual charity involved in this work. This whole question deserves considerably more attention than can be given it here, and I would suggest that those who give retreats to diocesan priests would do well to study the theological problems involved and bring home the truth to us, not just by pious exhortations but by a well thought out and theologically sound exposition of the relation between the prayer of the Church and our personal contribution. There I must leave the question and consider some further effects of the priest's outlook, of his role as minister of the sacraments.

Every priest engaged on missionary work is well aware of the struggle, painful at times, to keep the faith spoken of by Fr Schillebeeckx alive in his ministrations, to foster that hope that alone gives meaning to his work, to cherish that charity which ought to be its inspiration and which can sometimes be sorely tried in the day to day routine. No doubt this will be truer of less spiritually rewarding missions than ours here in Ireland. But even here discouragement and frustrations can take their toll.

In that struggle the priest can be helped considerably by a deeper realization of the true dimensions of his sacramental mission. If he refuses to allow his vision to be limited by the narrow bounds of his own parish or district, but looks instead to the wider expanse of Christ's Church, Christ on earth; if he sees himself and his people as actors in the eternal drama of God's saving love for men, and redeemed man's worship of God; then his solicitude for his "little flock" will acquire a new depth. Speaking recently of the late Pope's well-known love for people, the Archbishop of Dublin described it in the happy phrase "not mere human benevolence, but the charity of Christ". That is the ideal of every priest's love for his people, a love which will be none the less warmly human because it is built on the divine. But this love will be saved from the dangers of narrowness, of paternalism, of the "back-garden" mentality of mere parochialism only if it looks to broader horizons. And the priest who cultivates such a sublime view of his sacramental ministry will never run the risk of forgetting that this is his principal reason for being among his people; or the risk of pushing any other activity, no matter how praiseworthy, so zealously as to endanger the charity which is essential to his sacramental ministration. Every priest who has to deal with people is aware of the danger, inherent in his efforts for the good of his flock, of becoming involved in too narrow and parochial a way in their affairs; of acquiring what might be called a village mind, instead of the broad apostolic outlook proper to a priest; of being dragged down by his people rather than raising them up. Here too the right view of his sacramental ministry will save him from many pitfalls.

Again, this looking outwards towards the universal Church as the prolongation of Christ's mission on earth will have the further salutary effect that it will make the priest, in his ministrations to his people, sensitive to pastoral movements in the Church, as well as the interests of his own particular people. Too often a priest can get the idea that this parish is entirely his concern, that he knows best what is good for the people. The result can be an attitude of something very like resentment to directives or suggestions from above, the "why-can't-they-leave-things-alone" mentality that grumbles at every suggestion of change instead of seeing the pastoral possibilities of all these directives for achieving a more worthy or better understood celebration of the sacraments. There is no need to stress what a dangerous mentality that would be in these days of renewal in the Church.

Not only the priest's interior attitude but his external celebration of the sacraments will be deeply influenced by his regarding them as acts of Christ and his Church. If the sacraments are acts of Christ and his Church then it follows that they ought to be performed not according to the convenience, (much less the whim!) of the officiating priest, but according to the instructions laid down by Christ's Church. No right-thinking priest who understands the true nature of the sacraments will advocate that fastidious attention to details of rubrics which would make them ends in themselves. But it is to be feared that our national temperament and history incline us towards the opposite extreme. We give ourselves a sort of general dispensation from any strict adherence to the details of ceremonial, based on our past when the poverty of churches and church furnishings and the fewness of clergy made anything like a worthy performance of ceremonies difficult or impossible. We still take the short cut to validity (don't we even boast of the fact?) with the result that we deprive our ceremonies of much of their solemnity and of their power of impressing and instructing those who assist at them. It is just ninety-five years since a dean of Maynooth College wrote that "a great zeal for sacred ceremonies has been manifested throughout the country, especially since the Synod of Thurles. The improvement is still going on, and we may hope that many years will not elapse until every trace of the mutilation caused by the penal laws will have disappeared from our ritual observances". The progress of the intervening years can hardly be said to have justified the dean's optimism!

The Title in the Roman Ritual which I have already quoted reminds priests forcibly of their duty of a correct attitude to the rites of the sacraments by quoting the Council of Trent's anathema against anybody who holds that these rites can without sin be despised, omitted at will, or changed by any pastor of a church. Its own injunction is that these ceremonies should be performed *decenter gravique actione*—"becomingly and with a grave demeanour". On the question of the words used in the administration of the sacraments the Ritual, as we saw, distinguishes between those words which pertain to the form of the sacrament and the other prayers which surround it. In the form of the sacrament each word is to be pronounced "attentively, distinctly, piously and in a clear voice". With regard to the other prayers The Ritual contents itself with declaring that the minister "shall say them devoutly and religiously".

Here again while we admit the importance of ensuring validity, we must beware of the attitude of regarding the merely valid sacrament as the norm, with the consequent disregard for the ceremonies that surround its administration. If the sacrament is merely a thing which is brought into existence by the joining of matter and form as if by the throwing of a switch, then only the essential form is of any real importance. But if the sacrament is looked upon rather as an act, an act of Christ and his Church seeking for the response from man which will make it a real encounter in faith, then vestments, linens, candles, gestures and words have all of them their own importance in representing Christ's and his Church's grace-giving approach to man and in helping to elicit the appropriate response from man's soul. And the priest who mutiliates words or gesture or who shows himself ready without any justification to ignore these things and to substitute his own way of doing things for that prescribed by the Church, on the plea that it is all valid anyhow, —such a priest shows himself very insensitive to the true nature of the sacramental encounter.

So far we have considered chiefly the priest's responsibility to the sacraments themselves as acts of Christ and his Church. We have considered only incidentally his obligations to his people. We must now turn to this most important question. "To say that a sacrament is a gift of God is true but it is not enough", writes Fr Roguet. "It is also a step taken by man as he goes to meet his gift; it is this very meeting. It is not only . . . a call on

God's part, it is also man's response," We have spoken of the sacrament as an encounter with God. Man must bring to that encounter his faith and his longing to receive God's grace through Christ and his Church. He is not a passive recipient of God's favours in the sacrament, but must himself play an active part in its celebration. This is the full meaning of the phrase "not placing an obstacle". The dispositions of the recipient do not affect the validity of the sacrament: that is, Christ and his Church can show in the sacramental sign the desire for encounter with the soul, without any response being evoked on the part of the soul. That is what a merely valid sacrament is. But that is not what a sacrament is intended to be. To quote Fr Roquet again: "The great obstacle to a sacrament is 'fiction', that is to say, the lie of a person professing a faith that he does not truly possess". Every sacrament is a sign of faith, its celebration and its reception are a profession of faith.

It follows that the recipient of the sacrament, no less than the minister, is bound to bring his own personal contribution to the celebration of the sacrament. "The inner religious condition of the receiving subject", says Fr Schillebeeckx "is not merely a disposition which precedes or parallels the sacrament: it enters into the very essence of the fruitful sacrament".

This is of the utmost importance to the minister of the sacraments; because as we saw from the Roman Ritual the priest has the duty of striving, by his instruction and by the example of his own reverence for the sacraments, to foster in his flock the understanding of the sacraments and the faith in them that will enable the recipients to make their response to the sacramental sign offered them by Christ and his Church. A priest does not then fulfil his sacramental ministry merely by administering the sacraments. He will have to instruct his people on them.

The priest's instruction on the sacraments will be carried out principally in his preaching and catechetical instruction; where the opportunity exists he will also give some instruction on the occasion of the actual administration of the sacraments. Like every good teacher he will base his instruction on the needs of his hearers, on their intellectual capacity and their spiritual development. For example, the needs of an Irish congregation or class of school-children will be different from those of a similar group in countries where the reception of the sacraments is not the common practice and where social pressures militate against it. The *Directoire* to the French clergy which I have mentioned earlier has much to say of the problem of non-practising Catholics. In our country we have to deal with a situation in which sacramental practice is almost universal and is socially accepted. Our chief problem in dealing with our very small minority of non-practising Catholics will be the danger of forcing on them a mere external conformity with our wish that they should receive the sacraments. We have to make sure that there is some faith there.

For the rest our task will be to try to deepen our people's appreciation of the sacraments they frequent so faithfully. Their danger is that of thinking of the sacraments as an easy way to heaven, demanding of them no more personal effort than is involved in going to the Church and receiving them. It should, I think, be emphasized that the instructing of people on the sacraments is not entirely or even predominantly an intellectual process. The aim is not to train apologists but living, practising, witnessing Christians. And actually as you all know one does find at times in the unlearned a quite surprising perception of such truths. But the presence of that simple faith does not lessen the need for instruction.

The principal means of instruction for the general body of his people will always be the priest's Sunday sermon. In both this and the visit to the school it ought to be possible by frequent repetition to emphasize the essential nature of the sacrament as a personal encounter with God, demanding the commitment of faith and Christian living on man's part, rather than a magical rite ensuring salvation. The task of teaching this true sacramental outlook, as distinct from mere sacramental practice, is not an easy one. It would be considerably lightened if we had for our people—children and adults—a catechism on which we could base such instruction in church and school. Our present catechism —an excellent compendium of sixteenth-century theology in nineteenth-century English—is practically useless for this purpose. The sacraments are primarily facts not of philosophy or

theology but of history, biblical history; and of life, the everyday
life in Christ of redeemed man. Their language and ritual are
biblical, Christ-centred. Their relevance is for ordinary unlettered
folk as much as scholars. They speak of belief and love, not of
matter and form; they convey their message through bread and
wine and oil and the touch of men's hands, not through substance
and accidents. They come from One who taught not from a
rostrum but from a boat or on a hillside, and who healed and
blessed with the touch of his hand or the hem of his garment.
We cannot afford to allow the teaching and preaching of this
simple truth to become abstract, academic, scholastic, without
irreparable loss to the Christian life of our people. As Fr Godfrey
Diekmann has written ". . . if the vision of the whole is obscured,
Christian life becomes all too easily (and tragically) a *sum total*
of, say, 170 truths and 2414 laws. We lose sight of the fact that
Christianity is not so much a hundred or more facts, but one
sole fact, one sole all-embracing reality: Christianity is Christ,
the Son of God made man, living in and through his Body, the
Church".

I cannot appeal too strongly for a text-book—call it catechism
or what you will—for use in school and home which will present
the faith of Christ and the life of his members in his Church as
such a unified and inspiring vision. It would, I believe, be of
incalculable service in providing the background of knowledge
necessary for the appreciation of instruction on the sacramental
rites and formulae of the living worshipping Church. The presence
of such a background and of a standard text-book in schools
and homes would make the task of the preacher and teacher of
religion much lighter and, more important still, infinitely more
effective. I scarcely need add that such a knowledge, based not
on the abstract formulae of theology but on the living language
of faith and life, would be likely to prove a much better equipment and stronger defence for the young than their present
religious training.

The other great opportunity for instruction on the sacraments
is, as the Council of Trent and the Roman Ritual recommend,
the occasion of the actual celebration of the sacraments. Some of
the sacraments lend themselves to such instruction more than

others—for example, baptism and extreme unction. (The exhortation and instruction of penitents in the sacrament of penance is essentially the same thing). The immediate purpose for such instruction will be to secure worthy and devout celebration and assistance at the sacrament. The audience will be a much smaller one than that for the general instruction in the church, and the appeal of such instruction as is given will be correspondingly more personal and hence more effective. Brief and simple but forceful explanations of a ceremony or formula will be the aim of the priest.

The sacrament is a sign—a sign of grace, and a sign of faith, the faith of the Church and the faith of the persons taking part in the ceremony. Being a sign it ought to convey a message. But obviously it can convey a message only if it is understood. Hence the liturgy of the sacraments is supposed to be itself an instruction and an incentive to faith. The fact that the Reformers reduced the sacrament to being merely a sermon in action should not be allowed to obscure from us the fact that a sacrament really is just that, as well as being of course a good deal more. Unfortunately the language of symbolism and prayer contained in the sacramental ritual is no longer clear to the ordinary Christian, and what was originally the explanation of spiritual realities has itself now to be explained.

The permission to use the vernacular in many of the ceremonies of administration of the sacraments has been a significant step forward in putting the understanding of the ritual of the sacraments within the reach of the faithful. The publication in cheap booklet form of portions of this ritual makes the prayers available for all. There is no reason at present why a ceremony of baptism should not be preceded by a short instruction on the sacrament and the bystanders supplied with the text of its administration. People can also be made familiar with the Ritual for the care of the sick, the anointing, the burial service and the marriage rite.

The purpose of all such instruction ought to be to assist the understanding and piety of the faithful, so as to enable them to "worship in spirit and in truth", to take their part worthily in the encounter with God which a sacrament is, instead of being mystified listeners and onlookers as if they were the objects of some magical rite. "*Worship in spirit*", Fr Roguet says "does not mean a disembodied worship, but a worship where the ceremonies have a meaning, excite piety, suggest the mystery of God, raise up the soul and give it a sense of consecration instead of being confined to a mechanical administration, or unintelligible incantations. *Worship in truth* is a true preaching of the Gospel through the sacraments . . . It is a worship shorn of non-essentials, intelligent and intelligible, always preserving a due sense of the mystery involved; it is a worship that demands, not passive and stupefied spectators, but enlightened and active participators, formed by methodical and deeply religious instruction".

But there are difficulties about such instruction too, just as there are in the case of sacramental instruction in church and school. The first of these is precisely that lack of biblical background in the minds of the people which I referred to already. The Ritual introduces them into the world of patriarchs and prophets, of the Exodus, of Sion and its Temple. "Be bountiful, O Lord, to Sion in your kindness by re-building the walls of Jerusalem; Then shall you be pleased with due sacrifices, burnt offerings and holocausts; then shall they offer up bullocks on your altar"! For you and me such expressions as these are capable of conjuring up a picture of the Holy City and its Temple, even of raising our minds to the heavenly courts. I sometimes wonder what they meant for the poor old soul at whose sick-bed I spoke them on the one and only occasion when I ventured to use that particular part of the liturgy!

There is another and somewhat similar difficulty which the translation of the ritual of the sacraments has forced on our attention. I refer to the unsatisfactory nature of some of the prayers surrounding the administration of the sacraments. Ideally these prayers ought to give a clear and strong indication of the nature of the sacramental action and the spiritual fruit expected from its worthy performance. Undoubtedly there are such prayers —one might instance those surrounding the Communion of the sick or the marriage rite. But it must be confessed that there are others where no such happy note is struck. The baptismal service, for instance, while it contains some beautiful and expressive prayers and ceremonies, is lacking in any well-defined line of thought and is almost completely incomprehensible to anybody but a liturgical scholar. Another example of a notable weakness in our Ritual is the introduction to the anointing of the sick. The rubric leaves it to the priest in his own "pious words" to point out briefly the meaning of the sacrament and console the sick person, then the Ritual proceeds to fritter away these prayers on an entrance ceremony for the priest which has no particularly great spiritual value for the patient or the bystanders, and which is quite meaningless in the *ritus continuus* where the priest has already been in the house for a considerable time! It is to be hoped that we will see before very long such weaknesses and anomalies corrected, so that the Ritual can be used not merely as a ceremonial manual for the priest but as a source of instruction and edification for both priest and people.

There is yet another aspect of the sacraments which has been hinted at in many of the remarks made so far but which deserves some further consideration: that is their character as community worship. It is an aspect of which our people are largely unconscious and a great many of our clergy either unaware or—dare we say it?—suspicious. We tend to think, and to let our people think, of the reception of a sacrament as a private affair between the individual soul and God. We are conscious vaguely of baptism as incorporation into the Church, and perhaps of the social nature of the sacraments of holy orders and matrimony. What we fail to realise is that every sacrament is the affair of the whole community of God's People, the Church. The sacraments, as the French hierarchy's *Directoire* states, "express and realize incorporation into the Church. Signs of the Church, the sacraments are given in the community and with a view to the community, which they are destined to build up and bind together". It is difficult for the ordinary person to realise the sublime truth of his membership of the mystical body, harder still for him to bring this sublime truth down to the level of life by realizing the bond it sets up between him and his neighbours. And yet the realization of these truths may well be the most necessary condition for a healthy Christian life—as distinct from formal religious practice—among our people. It has been said that "our Irish spirituality is stronger in individual faith than in mutual charity".

Neither our preaching of the sacraments nor our celebration of them can be said to be of any great help to our people in this matter. A layman recently wrote of the conspiracy to conceal the doctrine of the mystical body from Irish Catholics, another described an Irish baptism "as the loneliest and dullest thing in the world".

If the sacraments are not merely remedies received from God, but also the communal worship of Christ's mystical body the Church, as has been so eloquently demonstrated by Pius XII in his encyclical on the Mystical Body and on Christian Worship, it is surely time that our instructions on the sacraments and our celebration of them began to show signs of these truths! Fr Roguet writes: "The clergy should direct their efforts to ensuring not only that the sacraments are administered under the conditions indispensable for validity, but also that they have their proper setting, in the framework of intelligent and communal piety".

The most obvious point at which to begin is the eucharistic sacrament-sacrifice,—the Mass and Holy Communion. This is not the place to enter into a discussion of community participation or the directives of the Church on the matter. It is the claim of the Liturgical Movement of our day that the rites of the Church can be made once again what they were intended to be, the prayer of the people as well as of the priest. For this, it holds, further education of the people will be necessary and also some modifications of the liturgy itself so as to make it more easily understood by people of our times, whatever their race or language. As you know, the discussion on the liturgy in the first session of the second Vatican Council was not really one of conservatives and liberals. It was rather a clash between this concept of the liturgy as something pastoral and therefore variable according to the needs of the people, and on the other side the idea of the liturgy as purely ritual and hieratic in character and therefore fundamentally static and unchangeable. Many of us see quite unnecessary and largely imaginary difficulties in these

THE PRIEST AS MINISTER OF THE SACRAMENTS

things, and because of our own prejudices fail to give our people the opportunity for a more intelligent and fruitful participation in the Mass. It is certain that they would be glad to avail of such helps and would benefit greatly from them.

The other sacraments too give opportunities for community celebration. Baptism need not be lonely or dull if the relatives are encouraged to participate in the ceremony and to understand its meaning. Communion and anointing of the sick are other occasions that can with very little instruction be turned into really moving ceremonies in which the family participates. The vernacular Ritual has made it possible for even the simplest people to make the responses and follow the ceremonies intelligently, or at least to grasp the fundamental idea that these are prayers and actions that concern not only the priest or the sick person but the rest of the household too. Here is a case where meticulous attention to rubrics is not necessarily the ideal. (I have one good parishioner who always answers my "Peace to this house" with the response "The same to you, Father"—which no doubt is deplorable rubrics, but I think excellent liturgy!)

Every sacrament is a meeting of the divine and human. It is the purpose of our sacramental ministry and therefore of our priesthood to bring about that meeting, to bring into the lives of our ordinary struggling people something of the infinitely sublime and incomprehensible life of God. It is a meeting that takes place in faith—the faith of the Church, the faith of the priest, the faith of the recipient of the sacrament. We must have that faith ourselves. We must also show our people that we have that faith. We must lead them too to an ever deeper and stronger faith, and a more enlightened faith that will prevent their reception of the sacraments from degenerating into formalism or superstition, or mere pious practice dissociated from the living of a true Christian life in all its aspects.

To stir up that faith in ourselves and in our people, to make our people realize that we have that faith ourselves, we have all the ceremonial of the sacraments and the attitude we show to them by such apparently trifling things as our proper vesting, our pronunciation of words, the dignity and impressiveness of our actions and gestures. We have the ministry of the word, which is inseparable from that of the sacraments. We have too the opportunity of encouraging devout and intelligent participation by our people in the ceremonial of the sacraments. Our task will be by the best use within our power of all these means to create the conditions in which the Redeemer can in the sacramental encounter pour out freely the graces he has won for his people.

We can never really say that we have exhausted these means. If the sacraments were merely things, even mysterious and sacred things, we might well reach a stage when we could say that we knew all about them that we were capable of knowing. But since a sacrament is not a thing but a personal encounter, then we can go on for ever learning about it, because we can never reach a complete knowledge of the persons involved. "We can understand a thing completely as long as we have enough intelligence", Mgr. Schmaus has said: "but we can perceive the inmost wishes, thoughts and will of a personal being only in as far as the personal being chooses to reveal himself to us". "To know a person", he adds, "we need a special faculty, not merely intelligence, but also love enlightened by understanding, a gaze warmed by love". To understand something more of the sacraments then we will have to turn our gaze on Christ their author and strive to understand something more of his redeeming love. We will have to turn "a gaze warmed by love" too on our people —not only on the devout and attentive, but on the lax, the careless and the ignorant. We shall need a special warmth of love for the sick who as they have their own sacraments provided for them by Christ and his Church have a greater claim than others upon our ministry.

And if we succeed in gaining a further insight into Christ and into those he wishes to lead through us to himself, perhaps we shall understand something more too of the third party involved —ourselves. And we shall realize that our availability for the sacramental ministry involves even more than a round-the-clock service—*quacumque diei ac noctis hora*—that it means a total giving of ourselves with all our talents and all our spiritual resources to the ministry which is our supreme task and our greatest privilege.

Bibliography

Bouyer, L., *The Word, Church and Sacraments*, London 1961.
The Paschal Mystery, London 1951.
Life and Liturgy, London 1956.
Rite and Man, London 1963.
de Bovis, A., *The Church, Christ's Mystery and Sacrament*, London 1961.
Callahan, D., Oberman, H., O'Hanlon, D. (Edd.), *Christianity Divided*, London 1962.
Casel, O., *The Mystery of Christian Worship*, London 1962.
Christian Worship, Encyclical Letter of Pope Pius XII *Mediator Dei*, London (C.T.S.) 1947.
Daniélou, J., *The Bible and the Liturgy*, London 1960.
From Shadows to Reality, London 1960.
Davis, C., *Liturgy and Doctrine*, London 1960.
Directoire pour la Pastorale des Sacrements, Paris 1951.
Fransen, P., *Faith and the Sacraments*, London 1958.
Graber, R., *Le Christ dans ses sacrements*, Paris 1947.
Häring, B., *Gabe und Auftrag der Sakramente*, Salzburg 1962.
Howell, C., *The Work of our Redemption*, Oxford 1953.
Leeming, B., *Principles of Sacramental Theology*, London 1955.
Palmer, P., *Sacraments and Worship*, London 1957.
Sacraments and Forgiveness, London 1960.
Philippon, M. M., *The Sacraments in the Christian Life*, Paris 1947.
Rahner, K., *The Church and the Sacraments*, Edinburgh-London 1963.
Theological Investigations II: Man in the Church, London 1963.
Roguet, A.-M., *The Sacraments, Signs of Life*, London 1954.
"Les sacrements en général", in *Initiation Théologique IV*, Paris 1961.
Schillebeeckx, E., *Christ the Sacrament*, London 1963.
Scheeben, M. J., *Le mystère de l'Èglise et de ses sacrements*, Paris 1956.
Semmelroth, O., *Die Kirche als Ursakrament*, Frankfurt 1955.
Le sens des sacrements, Brussels-Paris 1963.
Taymans d'Eypernon, F., *The Blessed Trinity and the Sacraments*, Dublin 1961.
Van Roo, W., *De sacramentis in genere*, Rome 1960.
Wegenaer, P., *Heilsgegenwart, die Heilswerk Christi und die Virtus Divina in den Sakramenten unter besonderer Berücksichtigung von Eucharistie und Taufe*, Münster-in-W 1958.